# I ALWAYS WONDERED ABOUT THAT

For further information, contact:
Tumblehome Learning, Inc.
201 Newbury St, Suite 201
Boston, MA 02116
http://www.tumblehomelearning.com

Library of Congress Control Number: 2017942023
ISBN 978-1-943431-29-8

Scheckel, Larry
I Always Wondered About That / Larry Scheckel - 1st ed

Cover Art: Barnas Monteith
Front cover science & technology icons: designed by Freepik from Flaticon
Front and back cover images: Courtesy NASA/JPL-Caltech (modified)

Printed in Taiwan

10 9 8 7 6 5 4 3 2 1

# I ALWAYS WONDERED ABOUT THAT

*101 Questions and Answers about Science and Other Stuff*

Larry Scheckel

TUMBLEHOME l e a r n i n g, Inc.

# *Dedication*

This book is dedicated to our grandchildren, Teddy and Marit Scheckel, who have been a constant source of joy to my wife, Ann, and me.

I take pride in the fact that I was able to teach these two grandchildren how to climb a tree fort, how take a drink of water from a running garden hose, how to get worms out of the ground with electricity, and how to ride a Spree motorcycle.

# Contents

## Three: The Science of Food and Drink

# Four: Remarkable People in Science

# Five : The Science of the Heavens and Earth

## Six: Art, Music, Sports, and Math

## Seven: Incredible Technology

## Eight: At the Fringes of Science

## Nine: The Magnificent Atom

## Ten: More Things I Always Wondered About

# Foreword

The strength of Larry Scheckel's writing and the influence it can have on both adults and kids is centered on his belief that everyone can enjoy and engage with the world around them. As a young university professor, I was searching for master teachers to inspire me and help me hone my craft. Seeing Larry present an hour-long workshop on sound, where he introduced me to countless eye-opening demonstrations, changed my thinking. I hastily scrawled notes, barely able to keep up with the word-play and crafting of stories; I struggled to capture his turn of phrase and interesting observations in hopes that I, too, could captivate an audience. I learned that one needs to inspire people to see the importance of and connectivity within the material before availing them to the interesting minutia of details. He taught me to care about teaching joy, teaching wonderment and teaching people that science is accessible to all.

What I saw that day is captured in this book. Sharing the joy of learning is a gift that many teachers possess, but Larry goes well beyond this simple idea by expanding his circle of sharing to include all ages and anyone asking interesting science questions. Through his written word he has moved beyond teaching kids the wonders of physics. He illuminates the world of science to the curious, to the inquisitive and to the questioning. This book evokes a sense of wonderment in its readers, bringing them back to the days of "but why" and "how does that work." Larry treats science as a brain teaser, setting you up to care about the question, but then revealing the answer in a way that the reader can have that "aha!" moment time after time.

This book can be pulled out and read in many different ways, cover to cover, shared oratory, or used in a classroom having students find their favorite story and report back to their peers, internalizing an interesting nugget of science to be shared with others. I have been known to pull his first book out while in my office with colleagues and ask for a number between 1 and 250 (the number of topics in the first book) and then open to the random topic, sharing a small tidbit of knowledge, and of the wonder of the world around us, with others. Today is the day for you to flip through the pages and find *your* "aha!" moments.

*Matthew Evans*
Professor, Physics & Astronomy
University of Wisconsin-Eau Claire

# Chapter One

# The Exquisite Human Body

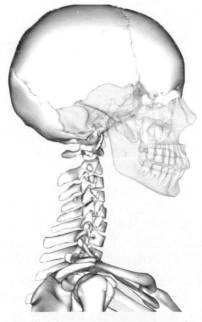

Wikimedia Commons :Rectus capitis anterior muscle

# Q1: How do they make those Magic Eye pictures?

A picture that has or appears to have height, width and depth is three-dimensional, or 3-D. A picture that has height and width but no appearance of depth is two-dimensional, or 2-D. Some pictures are 2-D on purpose. For example, think about the international symbols that indicate which door leads to a restroom. The symbols are designed so that you can recognize them at a glance. That's why they use only the most basic shapes.

We humans have two eyes, situated close together and side by side. That means that each eye sees a view from a slightly different angle. The brain takes information from each eye and unites them into one picture, interpreting the difference between the two views as depth. For objects up to about twenty feet (six to seven meters) away, the binocular vision system lets us easily tell with good accuracy the distance to an object.

Stereoscopic, or binocular, vision is vital to many human tasks, such as determining whether an object is moving toward or away from us, driving a car, threading a needle, or catching a ball. We could get along without 3-D vision, but life would be much harder.

Stereograms, called Magic Eye pictures, require the viewer to cross his eyes or look through the image and actually focus the eyes beyond or behind the picture.

The Magic Eye picture has a dot or pixel in two different positions on the print. The distance between the two pixels corresponds to how far back they seem to be when your gaze unites them in the picture. The size of the pixels, fading of color, and fuzziness all contribute to the depth of vision.

Some Magic Eye pictures have 2 dots or small circles printed above or below the picture. Stare at the two dots until you see 3 dots. Then move your gaze into the picture area. You should be able to see the hidden image. This method is sometimes called cross-eyed viewing.

There are other ways of ensuring that you can see those Magic Eye pictures. Hold the printed Magic Eye picture right up to your nose, and stare through it as if looking into the distance. Move the picture very slowly away from your face. Try not to blink or remove your gaze from the picture. The 3-D image will come into focus and the hidden image will appear.

There are several other ways of seeing 3-D, such as by using those red-blue glasses used to view picture books and comics. The old View-Master and "Honey, I Shrunk the Audience" at Disney World in Orlando use Polaroid glasses. The Pulfrich effect, in which one eye looks through a darkened lens and a stereo illusion occurs, was used during the Super Bowl half time in 1989, almost thirty years ago.

The latest development in 3-D technology is the wireless E-D glasses now used when playing some computer games. The electronic LCD glasses allow the left eye to see the image while the right eye's view is blocked. Then the right eye sees the image while the left eye is blocked. Vision goes rapidly back and forth between the two eyes, resulting in 3-D viewing.

## Q2: Why does your heart beat faster when you breathe faster?

Breathing rate (respiration rate) and heart rate (pulse rate) are two separate and different body functions. But they are related. We can't control our heart rate: it's automatic, controlled by nerves and hormones. We can control our respiratory rate, but there are backup and override systems to control it when we are asleep or not paying attention. Heart rate is largely an automatic function.

The respiratory rate is the number of breaths a person takes in a minute. For newborns, it's about 44 breaths per minute. Older children take 16-25 breaths per minute and an adult breathes 12 to 20 times per minute.

The pulse or heart rate is the number of times the heart beats in one minute. The normal resting heart rate for adults is about 72 bpm (beats per minute). It is higher for children, and lower for well-conditioned athletes.

When we work hard, such as running or swimming, the heart's blood flow increases to four or five times the flow that we have when we're inactive. The amount of blood pumped (cardiac output) is determined by the number of heart beats per minute (heart rate) times the amount of blood pumped with each beat (stroke volume).

When the heart is at rest and not working hard, the output is about five liters per minute. When the heart is working full blast, the output is about 20-25 liters per minute. (A liter is slightly more than a quart.)

If more blood is pumped, more oxygen must be supplied to the blood. Sympathetic nerves stimulate the respiratory muscles to increase the breathing rate. In addition, byproducts from muscles, such as lactic acid, hydrogen ions, and carbon dioxide stimulate the breathing centers in the brain, which in turn stimulate our respiratory muscles.

Higher blood pressure, caused by strenuous exercise, opens more air sacs (alveoli) in the lungs. The lungs put more oxygen into the bloodstream. In strenuous exercise, most every system in the body focuses on helping muscles do their work. A whole lot of systems are working together.

Breathing rate and heart rate are so automatic that we tend to pay little attention to them during our daily routine. But it is sobering to realize that we are all a few heartbeats away from eternity.

## Q3: How does oxygen get into your lungs?
. . . . . . . . . . . . . . . . . . . . . . . . . . . . . . . . . . . . . .

The lungs are wonderfully complex organs that absorb needed oxygen from the air for our body cells and get rid of the carbon dioxide that is the waste product of our cells. Breathing is one of our body's automatic activities. We breathe in and out about 12 to 25 times per minute and don't even think about it. Our breathing rate goes up when we exert the body, such as when we run or bicycle, and again we don't give the change a thought.

Oxygen and breathing are considered life essentials, in addition to food, water, warmth, and sleep.

Breathing involves an intricate plumbing system. The diaphragm is domed upward at rest. When we use muscular activity to inhale, or take in air, the diaphragm contracts and flattens, and the chest cavity expands. The diaphragm is the muscle at the bottom of the chest cavity that relaxes and contracts during breathing. This lowers the air pressure in the chest cavity. The higher pressure of the air outside the body pushes air into the mouth and nose, past the epiglottis, into the trachea (windpipe) and bronchial tubes and on into the lungs.

The epiglottis is a flap of tissue that closes over the trachea when we swallow so that food does not fall into the airways and obstruct our breathing.

Once it enters the lungs, the air passes into smaller and smaller tubes until it gets to the alveoli. The alveoli, or little air sacs, are where the real work of the lungs gets done. The average human has about 400 million of these tiny air sacs, and their surface area is about 750 square feet, or about half the area of a typical three-bedroom ranch house. It is in these tiny air sacs that a complicated gas exchange takes place.

Pulmonary capillaries surrounding each little air sac bring oxygen-poor and carbon dioxide-rich blood back from all parts of the body. This "used" blood must be replenished with oxygen and the carbon dioxide released.

In each air sac the oxygen concentration is high. Each red cell contains many copies of a molecule called hemoglobin, which can carry either oxygen or carbon dioxide. The hemoglobin in the red blood cells in the pulmonary capillary has carbon dioxide bound to it and very little oxygen. Oxygen passes (diffuses) through the membranes of the air sacs (alveoli) into the pulmonary capillaries. There the oxygen binds to the hemoglobin, displacing carbon dioxide, which in turn diffuses back into the alveoli. The carbon dioxide leaves those alveoli when we exhale. Meanwhile, the oxygen-rich blood is carried through the pulmonary veins to the heart. The heart pumps the oxygen-laden blood to all parts of the body. In the low-oxygen muscles and other tissues, oxygen diffuses out through capillary walls. The oxygen goes to feed the tissues, while waste carbon dioxide replaces it on the hemoglobin molecules.

It is a remarkable dance for the lungs whose job it is to keep their oxygen content high and carbon dioxide concentration low so that those air sacs can do a good gas exchange.

The medulla, or brainstem, is the site of the respiratory center. (Most of our automatic body functions, such as breathing, heart rate, and digestion are controlled by the medulla). The medulla automatically sends signals to the diaphragm to control breathing. It's like cruise control in a car.

There are special nerve cells in our airways that detect intruders, such as dust, pollen, water, cigarette smoke, and pollen. These guardian nerve cells send signals to the respiratory muscles to contract, causing us to sneeze or cough and violently expel the offending culprits.

At times, the respiratory centers go haywire and send too many impulses to the diaphragm. Hiccups are the term we use for these unwanted contractions of the diaphragm.

In any intricate and complicated mechanism things can go wrong. The lungs are no exception. Smoking is bad because particles coat the alveolar sacs, decreasing the surface area and preventing the needed exchange of oxygen and carbon dioxide.

Lots of people suffer from asthma, where the bronchial tubes constrict, reducing the size of the airways and causing people to wheeze. With emphysema, the lungs become stiff with fibers and less elastic. The lungs fail to empty well, making the muscles work harder. In bronchitis, the airways become inflamed and narrower, restricting airflow.

Carbon monoxide poisoning is dangerous. Carbon monoxide, a result of burning fossil fuels, clings to hemoglobin better than oxygen does. If carbon monoxide replaces oxygen in the blood, tissues will die of oxygen starvation. Too much carbon monoxide can bring on coma and death.

Go outside and deeply breathe in some fresh crisp air and think about all the apparatus at work in your lungs. Do resolve to take care of them.

## Q4: What happens to your brain and your body when you are sleeping?

. . . . . . . . . . . . . . . . . . . . . . . . . . . . . . . . . . . . . . . . . . .

We spend about one-third of our lives sleeping. A lot of things happen to us when we sleep. Body functions slow down. Heart rate drops. Breathing slows down. The amount of acid in the stomach decreases. The kidneys continue to filter waste, but at a slower rate. Blood flow to the brain is much less. Blood is diverted to the muscles.

There are five stages of sleep. The first four stages are regarded as quiet phases. Our brain cycles through the stages in approximately 90 minute intervals. The last stage is REM (rapid eye movement).

During the REM stage, there is a high level of brain activity. Our eyes move back and forth and up and down, as if we are trying to focus on something. During REM, parts of the brain we use for learning become very active. It is during the REM stage that we dream. Signals are sent to the motor neurons in the spinal cord. The muscles in the arms and legs become non-active, much like being paralyzed, so that we don't act on those dreams. During REM, blood flow to the brain increases to areas we use for memory and emotional experiences. Blood flow decreases to areas of the brain that are used for complex reasoning and language.

Sleep is a time for healing and for our body to do repairs. People who don't get enough sleep have difficulty thinking quickly, remembering details, or solving math problems. Poor sleep patterns are linked to poor health and lower life expectancy. There is evidence that lack of sleep reduces levels of white blood cells. This matters because white blood cells help fight infection. Sleep can restore our ability to fight infectious diseases. That's why you should rest when you're sick.

While we sleep, a cancer-killing protein molecule named TNF (tumor necrosis factor) pumps through our blood stream. If a person is sleep-deprived, TNF levels fall.

When we are awake, our bodies use oxygen and food to provide energy. More energy is spent than conserved. Energy is conserved during sleep, and repair and growth take over. Adrenaline levels drop, but the body produces the protein human growth hormone (HGH). All the tissues and bones of the body are undergoing growth, maintenance, and repair.

We humans have a built-in body clock called the circadian rhythm. Circadian means "about a day." Our circadian rhythm causes 24-hour changes in many body activities and governs the daily alternation between sleep and waking. It lets the body know when sleep is coming. The circadian rhythm regulates all the processes of the body by controlling a network of chemical messengers and nerves. Getting regular periods of sleep at night helps the body clock regulate hormone production.

Among other changes, body temperature falls during the night. By morning, body temperature is about two degrees Fahrenheit lower than in early evening. A person changes sleep position several dozen times during the night, but the muscles remain relaxed.

Sleep apnea is a disorder in which a person has abnormal pauses in breathing while asleep. These pauses can last from a few seconds to minutes. Sleep apnea is diagnosed with an overnight sleep test. If sleep apnea is not treated, serious medical problems can develop, such as headaches, daytime sleepiness, high blood pressure and dangerous heart rhythms.

## Q5: Is there a machine that can replace your real heart?

Yes, mechanical hearts exist, but they have limitations and problems. An artificial heart is a mechanical pump device that temporarily replaces the human heart. There is no "put it in and forget about it" artificial heart designed for long term use.

In 1982, a 61-year-old dentist, Barney Clark, became the first human to receive a permanently implanted artificial heart. It was known as the Jarvik-7 after its inventor, Dr. Robert Jarvik. Barney Clark lived 112 days after his operation. The second artificial heart recipient, William Schroeder, suffered a series of strokes but lived 620 days after he received a Jarvik-7 mechanical heart in November, 1984.

The power supplies for the Jarvik-7 resembled farm milking machines. Two large plastic tubes went through the patient's chest wall and were connected to a small refrigerator-size unit that did the pumping. Patients with a Jarvik-7 had no freedom of movement.

Today's artificial hearts are much more compact. The FDA has approved several implanted artificial hearts to serve as bridges to human heart transplant. SynCardia and AbioCor are two of the most mentioned names. Both systems are fully implanted inside the body. A rechargeable battery is implanted inside the patient's abdomen. This internal battery is charged via two coils, one internal and one external to the body. Power is transmitted via magnetic force across the skin without piercing the surface.

The advantage of this method of power delivery is that there are no wires or tubes coming out of the body. This technique lowers the chance of infection and allows greater patient movement. The external unit is a radio transmitter, and the receiver is a part of the pacemaker. The "recharging through the body" permits the person an hour to get up out of the bed, take a shower, or walk the dog before going back to get a recharge.

Thus far, about 1,000 people have received the SynCardia artificial heart. The SynCardia heart is a total heart, in that all four chambers are replaced. The AbioCor replaces the ventricles of the heart, the lower half of the heart. The heart's original atria are still intact and used. This approach works because the left ventricle does the majority of the heart's work, pumping blood to all parts of the body.

People diagnosed with heart failure live five years on average. To extend their life they will need a transplant or artificial heart. Heart failure causes 40,000 deaths per year, yet only about 3,000 hearts are transplanted each year. You can see that the need for human hearts greatly outpaces the supply. This makes a totally self-contained implanted mechanical heart a high priority item.

There are a number of problems to overcome to get a true "put it in and forget about it" mechanical heart. The power needed to operate a mechanical heart is substantial. It is much more than a pacemaker, which requires very little power. The heart is a pump, but not the kind of pump we use in our homes and cars. Normal pumps have impeller blades and can't be used in an artificial heart. Impeller blades would crush the red blood cells. Artificial hearts use hemispherical diaphragms that inflate and deflate to move the blood. If the seams and valves are in places where blood will clot, these clots can later break loose and cause life-ending strokes.

Rejection is another problem. The body tends to reject anything that is not "home grown." Some parts of newer machines are made from chemically treated animal tissues or biomaterials.

Skumin syndrome, another problem, is a mental disorder developed by 25 per cent of all patients who get an artificial heart, or even a valve replacement. With persistent doubts about the reliability of the devices and fear of the device breaking down, these patients suffer anxiety and depression. There is something very disconcerting about feeling and hearing that pump working inside of them.

## Q6: Why is there a big E on the top of the eye chart?

. . . . . . . . . . . . . . . . . . . . . . . . . . . . . . . . . . . . . . . . . . . . . . . .

We can credit Dr. Hermann Snellen, a Dutch ophthalmologist at the Netherlands Hospital for Eye Patients, with putting the big E on top, in 1862. He succeeded a Dr. Donders, who had done extensive research and developed complicated formulas for vision based on three parallel lines.

Snellen was trying to come up with a simple and standardized test for visual acuity to determine how good a person's eyesight was. He examined every letter of the alphabet, but only the letter E had three horizontal limbs separated by equal amounts of white space. There was also a one-to-one ratio between the height of the letter and the width of the letter, i.e., it was square. The gaps and bars of the E were all the same length. In most modern Snellen Eye Charts, the middle bar is shorter.

Vision specialists today use a version of the Snellen Eye Chart with eleven lines of letters. It seems that a lot of research has gone into making the letters. Each letter is called an optotype. Optotypes have a special geometry in which the height and width of each letter is five times the thickness of the line. And the thickness of the line is the same thickness as the white space between lines and the thickness of the gap between the cusps or ends in the letter C.

In a typical eye exam, the patient covers one eye and reads the letters. The smallest row that can be read from 20 feet (6 meters in most countries) demonstrates the visual acuity of the eye.

Snellen specified that a person with "standard vision" should be able to read the letter when it subtends 5 minutes of arc. That's the angle between the top and bottom of the letter as seen by the test subject. That would be one-twelfth of a degree. There are 360 degrees in a circle.

A person with normal vision is said to have 20/20 vision. Such a person can read at 20 feet what most persons can read at 20 feet. People with 20/10 vision have exceptional vision, because they can read at 20 feet what most people can read when only ten feet away. And 20/40 vision is not too good, because that person has to be at 20 feet away to see clearly what most people can see from 40 feet.

The definition of legally blind is now "with your best visual correction, you cannot read any letter on the 20/100 line in your better seeing eye, or you have a visual field diameter of 20 degrees or less in your better eye."

Several variations on the Snellen chart exist. In 1959, Louise Sloan came up with a widely used modification. Her Sloan chart, debuting in 1959, uses only 10 letters: C, D, H, K, N, O, R, S, V, and Z.

There is a special eye chart for illiterate adults and young children who cannot identify letters. The block letter of E is turned in different orientations or directions. With the "tumbling E" chart, the test subject points in which direction the E is facing.

The Landolt C eye chart is similar, using rows of the letter C. The tested person indicates which way the gap is facing. The Landolt Chart came out in 1888.

Eye specialists also have eye scanning devices that closely approximate a prescription for people who are physically unable to respond. That category might include infants, stroke patients, and head injury victims.

The most common vision defects are the well-known, near-sightedness (myopia), farsightedness (hyperopia), astigmatism, and presbyopia. Fortunately, these deficiencies can be corrected with eyeglasses, contacts, or laser surgery. It is nice to know that even if our eyesight is failing, we can always get that top row right!

## Q7: Why are some people color blind and what exactly do these people see?

Total color blindness is extremely rare but many people have difficulty telling certain colors apart. The most common type of color blindness is the inability to distinguish between red and green.

Light enters the eye through the cornea, lens, and eye fluid, and hits the retina, a meshwork of tightly packed nerve cells at the back of the eye. When specialized receptors in these nerve cells absorb light, nerve impulses fire and electrical signals travel to the brain via the optic nerve. The center of the retina is lined with three specific kinds of nerve cell receptors, called cones, that respond to red, green, and blue light. Red-green color blindness occurs when eyes lack red receptors.

Color blind people learn to compensate for their defect by associating certain colors with changes in the brightness of the light. Therefore, many color blind people don't know they have the defect. That's why we take those colored dot tests at the driver's license bureau.

Color blindness is hereditary and is caused by a recessive gene on the X chromosome. Only one healthy or dominant gene is needed for correct color vision. Girls get an X chromosome from each parent, so they can get a "normal" color vision gene from either parent. A boy, on the other hand, gets an X chromosome from his mother and a Y chromosome from his father. If the X chromosome from his mother carries the recessive, color blind gene, there is no other copy of the "normal" gene to make up for it, and the boy will be color blind.

About 8% of men are colorblind, and about one-half of one percent of women are colorblind. Color blind men cannot pass on the condition to their sons, since they pass on only a Y chromosome, not an X, to their son. However, the daughter of a color blind man will carry a gene for color blindness on one of her X chromosomes. Her other X chromosome is likely to carry a normal, or dominant, version of the gene. In order for a girl to be color blind, she must receive a recessive X from the mother and a recessive X from the father. That rarely happens, so colorblindness is sixteen times more prevalent in boys compared to girls. Colorblindness is not contagious.

There is something relatively new on the market—EnChroma™ glasses that are effective for four out of five  cases of the red-green color vision deficiency. Results depend on the type and extent of color vision deficiency.

What are the primary colors anyway? In grade school, children sometimes learn that the primary colors are red, yellow, and blue. Actually, we should use the terms, magenta (a light shade of red), yellow, and cyan (a light shade of blue). Magenta, yellow, and cyan are the primary colors for the subtractive process of pigments, paints, and printing.

The subtractive color process involves the mixing of dyes, inks, and paint pigments to create a wide range of colors. Each dye, ink, or pigment partially or completely subtracts, or absorbs, some wavelengths of light and not others. The color that a surface displays depends on which parts of the visible spectrum are not absorbed and therefore remain visible.

The primary colors for light are red, green, and blue. When we mix them together, we get white light. These are the colors we use for vision and for color television.

## Q8: Why can we see things in the dark by using our peripheral vision better than when looking straight at them?

When we see something out of the corner of our eye, it's called peripheral vision. Peripheral vision refers to the part of our vision outside the very center of our gaze.

Here is a quick review on how the eye works. Light passes through the outer layer of the eye called the cornea, goes through a clear liquid solution termed the aqueous humor, and passes through the pupil, or the black hole of the eye, to reach the lens. The cornea and lens bend or refract light. The light passes through the eyeball filled with a second liquid (vitreous humor) and then strikes the retina.

The image is formed on the retina in the back of the eye. The retina is like the film in a camera. This is where seeing takes place.

There are two types of receptors that make up the retina: rods and cones. Cones are found near the center of the retina and detect color. An easy way to remember this is to use the three Cs; center, cones, color. Most of our vision makes use of the densely packed cones in that center part of the eye, called the fovea. That fovea gives us color and fine detail.

The rods are found on the edges or periphery of the retina. Rods are far more numerous than cones. They are also a thousand times more sensitive to light, but they do not respond to color. A typical pair of eyes has six million cones and 120 million rods.

In dim light, at night, or in the dark, the cones are fairly useless. They are just not sensitive enough to respond to the low light. Since the rods are present at the extremes of the eye, we can better pick up objects by averting our glance rather than viewing them directly. As a matter of fact, hunter safety courses and military trainers say not to look directly at an object at night if you want to see it. Peer or scan around the object you are trying to see, so that the light falls on the rods. These trainers also teach how to maintain dark adaptation. It takes five to twenty minutes for the eyes to adapt from bright sunlight to complete darkness. For this reason, soldiers are trained to keep one eye closed while using a flashlight to read a map.

Consider these additional thoughts. We see a car in the far distance. We know it is a car, but can't quite make out the color of the car. Cars far away are dimly lit, or to put it more correctly, reflect very little light to us.

The brightness of an object is established by the inverse square law. This means the brightness of the object varies with one over x squared, where x is the distance to the object. An object twice as far away is one over two squared (four), so one-fourth as bright. An object three times farther away is one over three squared (nine), so one-ninth as bright.

The same is true with trees at a distance. They don't reflect light as brightly, so we see them primarily with our rods. Although we know they are green, our rods see them as grayish, and artists paint them as such.

Peripheral vision is important for functioning in everyday life. We see danger in "the corner of the eye," such as a car approaching as we cross the street. Sports people use peripheral vision constantly to spot their players and opponents. A chess player may look at a particular piece on the board, but her peripheral vision takes in the entire board.

Many animals, including dogs, have a difficult time seeing stationary objects. They see movement. Their eyes are packed with rods, but very few cones.

## Q9: Why is it so hard for us to float in water?
· · · · · · · · · · · · · · · · · · · · · · · · · · · · · · · · · · · · · · · · · ·

Well, the short answer is that we're too dense! Density is how heavy something is compared to the space it takes up. Put another way, density is the amount of mass in a given volume. Density is mass divided by volume, if we put it in a formula.

The human body is just slightly denser than either freshwater or salt water. There are a few bodies of water that are so salty that you can actually float in them easily. The Great Salt Lake in Utah is one. Mono Lake in California is another.

Water tries to hold up solid objects. If an object is too heavy for its size, it will sink. An object that is heavy for its size is said to have a high density. You and I sink because we are too heavy for our size or volume. We would float if we could stay the same size but didn't weigh as much. We would also float if we could stay the same weight, but developed a greater volume.

Muscle has a density greater than water and fat has a density slightly less that water. Bone density is considerably higher than muscle. Fat people can float better than skinny people. The overall density of fat people is slightly less than that of their skinny friends. That is a nice advantage of being a few pounds above the norm.

The human body is so close to water density, that if we fill our lungs with air and hold our breath, we can float. When we exhale, we sink. This is the basis of survival floating, where people can bob up and down for hours.

Drowning victims sink because their lungs fill with air, and their overall density is greater than that of water. They rise again after a few days as bacteria produce gas and make the body less dense than water.

Try this experiment. Guess whether these objects will float or sink: rock, orange, apple, wood stick, nail, bar of soap, and pencil. Put the objects in a bowl or pail of water. Objects that have too much weight for their size will sink.

Here is a neat one. Put a diet pop or soda in a container of water, such as a pail. Will it float or sink? Then put a regular pop or soda in the same container of water. Will it float or sink?

The regular pop will sink because it contains sugar. The regular can of pop is slightly denser than water.

The Diet, Lite or sugar-free can of pop will float. It is slightly less dense than water. The lack of sugar makes a difference.

Here's another one for you! Put an orange in a pail of water. It will float. It is less dense that water. Now peel the orange, and place the orange in water. It will sink. Put the peelings, or rind, in water. They float. The peelings increase the volume or an orange without appreciably increasing the mass. The orange peel acts like a life jacket, and it is why life jackets are worn when we go in the water.

## Q10: Why was Abraham Lincoln so tall and gangly?
· · · · · · · · · · · · · · · · · · · · · · · · · · · · · · · · · · · · · · · · · · · · ·

Medical people think that Lincoln suffered from Marfan syndrome. It is a rare inherited degenerative disease of the connective tissue. Marfan syndrome is named after Antoine Marfan, a French pediatrician who described the condition in 1896.

Marfan syndrome sufferers can have deformed chests and curvature of the spine (scoliosis). The bones grow abnormally long, so people with Marfan syndrome tend to be unusually tall. In a normal person, arm span equals height. But people with Marfan syndrome can have arm spans greater than their heights. Sometimes these people will have heart murmurs because of defects of the aorta and heart valves. The lungs may be affected. The dural sac around the spinal cord may be challenged. Marfan syndrome people tend to be very nearsighted.

Scientists discovered the gene that is responsible for Marfan syndrome in 1989. They found that the syndrome is inherited by a dominant trait, carried by the FBN1 gene on chromosome 15. Since the gene is dominant, a person with Marfan syndrome may have inherited it from either parent.

Marfan syndrome is diagnosed by a series of tests, including echocardiogram, electrocardiogram, and a slit lamp eye test. The slit lamp eye test helps the doctor determine if the lenses in the eye are dislocated or out of place. A CT scan or MRI of the lower back can also help in the diagnosis. There is a genetic blood test for Marfan syndrome, but it is very complicated, expensive, and subject to some limitations.

Larry Scheckel

Note that Marfan syndrome suffers might have lung capacity issues. You can try measuring your own lung capacity. Fill a gallon milk carton with water, invert it and put it in a pan, bowl or sink of water. Insert a tube or small hose into the opening of the carton. Take a deep breath and blow through the tube, emptying the air from your lungs as completely as possible. Mark the water level on the side of the carton with a piece of tape. Empty and remove the milk carton, turn it right side up, and fill the milk carton to the level of the tape. This is the amount of air you blew into the milk bottle. You have just measured your vital lung capacity.

By the way, not everyone would consider Lincoln ugly. Some might say that Abraham Lincoln was "ruggedly handsome"!!

# Chapter Two

# Animals
## *All the Creatures on Earth*

## Q11: *How do animals protect themselves from predators?*

Animals have developed numerous remarkable defenses to keep from being devoured by their enemies. They hide, they flee, they confuse or threaten their predator, or they fight back.

Animals can change their color to match their surroundings. The arctic fox has grey fur in spring and summer. As fall and winter approaches, the fur changes to white, matching the color of snow. The chameleon and iguana change skin color to match their background. Camouflage is a powerful tool in the animal kingdom.

The daddy-long-legs spider has a long, thin body that looks like a stick or twig. Its color blends in with trees and branches. Leaf insects are hard to spot as they merge in with the green leaf. Squids emit a black ink to hide themselves in the water.

Grazing animals will feed in herds. Deer, buffalo, and zebra fall into this category. They scatter when attacked, confusing their pursuers. Other animals confuse their predators by changing their behavior. The opossum will play dead. Some beetles and millipedes also fake death. The killdeer pretends it has a broken wing to lure predators away from its young.

Many animals have a keen sense of hearing, smell, and sight. They survive by running or flying away. In some animal groups, certain individuals act as sentries to warn their fellows of danger. For example, crows, prairie dogs, and meerkats all have special calls to warn of predators.

There is a whole category of animals, such as garden snails, tortoises, crabs, and clams that are covered by hard shells. Clams close up their shells. The tortoise or turtle can pull in its head and legs for greater protection.

Porcupines and starfish have needles or spines to ward off enemies. The sting of poison protects wasps, scorpions, centipedes, and some snakes. Skunks spray attackers with a horrible smell.

Some creatures use horns or antlers to fend off predators. Tigers, raccoons, and bears have extremely sharp claws and teeth that discourage others from messing with them. The venom of a daddy-long-legs kills most of its predators, though it is harmless to humans.

A few creatures don't taste good to their foe. Many of these have bright colors to let their enemies know they are not worth eating. Sea slugs and monarch butterflies are prime examples.

Animals that find ways to protect themselves and live long enough to have families will survive. Creatures that do not find such means will be killed off by their enemies. It's a cruel world out there!

## Q12: *Do stingrays really sting?*

A stingray fatally stabbed Steve Irwin in the heart on September 4, 2006 while the famed Australian "Crocodile Hunter" was filming segments for his television program. A few weeks later, a stingray jumped into a fishing boat in Florida and stabbed an 81-year-old man in the chest. The barb penetrated James Bertakis's heart. But unlike Irwin, Bertakis did not try to pull the saw-like stinger out. A close call, but Bertakis survived.

The stingray that dealt Steve Irwin a life-ending blow was an Australian bull ray believed to be about six feet long and weighing 200 pounds. This stingray had a stinger about eight inches long located at the base of the tail. Stingrays have one or more barbed spikes on the tail. The length of that serrated spike is from four to ten inches, and the underside has two grooves with venom glands.

Stingrays have flat bodies that allow them to conceal themselves. They agitate the sand and hide beneath the cloud they create. Their eyes are on top of their bodies and their mouths are underneath, so stingrays can't see their prey. They rely on smell and electro-receptors similar to sharks' to navigate and find their prey. They feed around coral reefs.

Cases like Steve Irwin's are very rare. Usually, stingrays are docile. They do not normally attack humans, but will protect themselves if stepped on. The stinger causes pain and muscle cramps from the poison. The poison is not life threatening.

A stingray must face its victim when it attacks. It flips its long tail upward over its body so it hits whatever is in front of it. The sting or barb enters a person smoothly, but the exit can be rough. It has been compared to those "severe tire damage" spikes around rental car agencies, which strongly deter a driver from backing up. Most stingray jabs strike humans around the feet, and it usually takes a doctor to remove the stinger from the victim's flesh.

Certain tourist areas, like Grand Cayman Island, Antigua, and Belize, allow visitors to swim with and feed the stingrays. Mother stingrays bear live young in litters of six to twelve; therefore, the population in tourist areas is quite high. There are many companies that offer stingray trips, making it a top tourist attraction in the large, shallow reserves where the rays live. Snorkeling is possible and the stingrays are used to the presence of humans. Injuries are very rare.

People, especially in the Far East, eat stingrays. The most prized part is the wings, properly called flaps. Stingray chefs grill it over charcoal and serve it with spicy sambal sauce. Nyonya's, a Malaysian restaurant in Chinatown, New York City, is well-known for its stingray delicacies.

## Q13: *How do dogs know what you're saying when you're training them?*

. . . . . . . . . . . . . . . . . . . . . . . . . . . . . . . . . . . . . . . . . . . . . . . . . .

A dog's mental abilities compare to those of a human child between two and two-and-a-half years old. There is a huge difference between breeds when it comes to dogs' ability to learn and to process information. If we consider trainability as a sign of intelligence, the Border Collie is considered top dog.

Dogs do learn differently from humans. According to a recent study by Yale University, babies associate a word with the shape of an object. Dogs, instead of shape, focus on size and texture.

The average dog can learn about 165 words. Dog IQ tests consist of testing their ability to recognize and fetch a particular toy from a pile of toys. The dog learns to pair a word with a particular object. One really smart Border Collie learned over 1,000 words.

A big problem is that we don't know how dogs process information. If we give a dog a certain command, such as "sit" or "roll over," the canine may be responding to our body movements as much as to the word. Or the dog may be responding to a past reward associated with the command.

The word "sit" may not have the same meaning when used at a different location or spoken by a different person, or given in a different tone of voice. A lot of research shows that dogs do respond primarily to our body language, even our unconscious body language, and even very subtle signals such as our eye movements. Current research seems to indicate that humans and dogs have co-evolved for so long together that dogs understand some gestures (like a person pointing at an object) that wolves and even much more intelligent animals, like chimps, don't get.

The first step in training a dog is to get the dog to turn and look at you when you call his or her name. Say the name in a clear voice, and immediately afterward reward the dog with a treat or toy. Repeat a dozen times with a wait after each time. While the dog is looking away, call its name. If it turns and looks at you, say "Yes," and reward it with a treat. Before long, your dog will know its name. The next step is to have the dog come to you when its name is called.

I had a mutt (mixed breed) dog when I was a kid on the farm. I loved that dog, but once I tried a little experiment. I said to Browser, in an upbeat sing-song voice, all the while smiling and stroking his head and ears, "You are a really bad dog." Browser wagged his tail and moved closer, thinking I had praised him. He was responding to tone of voice, not actual words.

We mentioned the Border Collie as top dog for intelligence and a real workaholic as a sheep herder. We recently watched in awe as a Border Collie worked a sheep herd in New Zealand. Poodles, Dobermans and German Shepherds also rank high in intelligence. Dobermans and German Shepherds, because of their high dog IQ, are in demand as police dogs and military guard/war dogs. Both breeds make good pets.

Beagles and hounds, and northern breeds like huskies, were bred to work independently, using their own instincts, and don't do so well in obedience training.

Dogs are very expressive animals. They communicate feelings of fear, sadness, happiness, and nervousness better than most animals, certainly better than cats. Most breeds of dogs are very eager to please, and I suppose that's why they're known as man's best friend.

## Q14: Why are some dogs afraid of thunderstorms?

There seems to be no good explanation why some dogs are afraid of storms while most are not. Some dogs are fearful of the thunder, but dogs may also be affected by lightning, a drop in the barometric pressure, or a change in the electrostatic or electric field. Some experts believe that fear of thunderstorms starts with the fear of noise, any noise. The loud thunderclaps can escalate a dog's fear and a phobia of most any sound.

Certain dog breeds seem to be more susceptible to fear of thunderstorms. Collies, German Shepherds, Beagles, and Basset Hounds are the most influenced. Dogs that have separation anxiety are more likely to have noise and thunderstorm phobias.

Canine behavior experts recommend that dog owners not comfort their pet in a sympathetic voice when their pet acts afraid. It can make the dog feel there is really something to fear. They suggest using a happy, jolly, hearty voice instead. Also, they say that the owner shouldn't exhibit any nervous tendencies dogs can pick up on. Nor should the dog be punished for showing fear. That will only make it worse.

Vigorous exercise of their dogs prior to a storm is effective for some dog owners because it can tire the pooch out.

Vets recommend that you provide the dog with a safe place to go during a storm, perhaps an inside room that is quiet, a basement, or a dog crate. Some dogs do better if there is background noise, such as music or television.

Some dogs may need medication to cope with a storm. Typical medications prescribed by the vet might include Xanax, Elavil, Buspar, Valium, and Prozac. Valium would be a drug that acts rather quickly, while Prozac might take several weeks.

We had several dogs on the farm I grew up on. "Boots," a beautiful long-haired black-and-white mutt, mostly collie, ran for the basement steps at the first inkling of a storm. Her fears were misplaced. She got run over by a pickup truck. Doggone!

## Q15: *How can a cat, dropped upside down, land on its feet?*
. . . . . . . . . . . . . . . . . . . . . . . . . . . . . . . . . . . . . . . . . . . . . . . . .

The cat's marvelous ability to land on its feet never ceases to amaze people. The cat needs about two to three feet of falling distance. Time lapse photography has been used to carefully study the cat's motion. The main science principle involved is conservation of angular momentum.

Ice skaters exhibits conservation of angular momentum when they do a pirouette. The skaters start with arms and legs stretched out from the body and give a slight rotation motion. Then, they rapidly bring the arms and legs inward close to the body. Their rotation rate increases and they spin rapidly. The conservation of angular momentum basically says that if you decrease the radius of the mass (bring mass inward), you increase the spin rate.

Analyzing the cat's motion can be quite complex. Think of the cat as consisting of two halves-the front half and the rear half. The front half is turned or righted first. The cat draws in its paws, making the turn easier to make. Objects spin or rotate more easily when the mass is close to the axis of rotation. At the same time, the hind legs are extended outward. The cat then rotates its front half.

To make the angular momentum zero, the rear half must rotate in the opposite direction. But the rear half has the mass further from the center of rotation, meaning it does not have to rotate so far to balance the rotation of the front half.

Once the front half is rotated, the rear haunches then swing around in the same direction that the head rotated. The cat now extends its forepaws, draws in the rear legs, and rotates the rear half in the same direction that the front half rotated during the first stage of the process. Now the front half rotates somewhat in the opposite direction but not as much as the rear. So a total net rotation is achieved, and the cat lands right side up. The tail helps in the rotation, but even tailless cats can land right side up.

You might want to try this example of the conservation of angular momentum principle. Spin a hard-boiled egg on a smooth surface, such as a kitchen counter or tabletop. Notice the egg started from a 'lying down' position and went to a "standing on its head" position. The spinning hard-boiled egg has to maintain constant angular momentum. If it has a rapid rotation rate, then it has to decrease its radius or width to compensate. The egg rises up against gravity to move its mass closer to the axis of rotation.

## Q16: *Do horses sleep standing up?*

This question was a source of endless argument for the three Scheckel brothers growing up on the farm outside of Seneca, Wisconsin. We never did come to any definitive conclusion. We even snuck out of the house one summer night and went to the barn to witness if Dolly, Prince, and Lightning were standing in their stalls or lying down. All three were standing, but we couldn't figure out if they were sleeping or awake.

Veterinarians say horses have a suspensory ligament apparatus in the lower leg that locks up. Because their legs can lock in place, horses can fall asleep without falling over. So, it turns out horses do sleep standing up and horses also sleep lying down.

Historically, horses were prey for wildcats, lynx, and mountain lions, and could not sleep safely on the ground. Horses have straight backs, so they cannot get up quickly. If an enemy mountain lion were to come along while a horse was on the ground, it might not be able to get up fast enough to make an escape.

In the wild, horses only lie down in a herd while a select few opt to remain upright. It is their defense designed to protect the herd from predators. Horses are at their "weak" moment and more vulnerable to attack when on the ground.

When a horse stands still, it is able to relax, so there is little fatigue. If necessary, a horse can remain upright for several days before it lies down. Horses do occasionally take short naps lying down during the day. This helps them to rest their legs. You can sometimes find a horse stretched out on its side, asleep in the sun, or lying on the ground with its legs folded under. However, horses don't stay lying down for long. Pressure on their rib cages makes it too difficult for them to breathe. Average lying-down time for a horse is about 30 minutes.

A ligament is a strong flexible connective tissue that joins bone to bone. They are parallel bundles of collagen fibers. We humans have something akin to the horse. We have a suspensory ligament that holds the lens in the correct place in our eye.

Warning: a sleeping horse should not be disturbed. A startled horse may kick.

## Q17: *What color is the skin of a polar bear?*

The polar bear's skin color is actually black. Bear hair, or fur, is nearly colorless, but it appears white because visible light is reflected from the rough inner surface of each hair. Each hair on the bear acts as an optical fiber that carries heat from the sun to the skin. The secret is total internal reflection. Like light in an optical fiber, the radiant energy bounces around inside of the hair, much like a bullet that ricochets down a steel pipe.

The dark skin of the bear absorbs the light rays. The long, coarse outer guard hairs are hollow and air-filled. Hairs of the thick undercoat are not hollow. The hairs are not entirely transparent, but slightly off-colored because they contain keratin. Keratin is the same kind of material that makes up our fingernails and toenails.

Polar bears love cold weather. They can swim in ice-filled sea water in great comfort. That very thick undercoat of hair prevents water from soaking the bear skin. Bears are in more danger from overheating (hyperthermia) than from freezing (hypothermia).

Chasing a seal at four miles per hour, a polar bear's temperature can reach a dangerous 100 degrees Fahrenheit. The polar bear may have to stop and lie on its back with paws up in the air, just to cool down. That's why polar bears prefer to sit by a hole and wait for their dinner to come to them.

You kids can put on a latex glove and stick your hand in a bucket of ice water. That hand gets cold in a hurry. Now place some lard or shortening in the glove, or coat your hand with lard or shortening. Place your coated hand in the ice water. Notice the insulating value of the lard or shortening.

What color is a polar bear? Underneath that black skin is a thick layer of fat. That layer of lard insures a comfortable and happy bear. So in essence, a polar bear is black and white and warm all under!

## Q18: When you shine a light on deer at night, why do their eyes light up?

. . . . . . . . . . . . . . . . . . . . . . . . . . . . . . . . . . . . . . . . . . . . . . .

The round black center of our eye is the pupil. The pupil is actually a hole that lets light into the eye. The pupil is like the diaphragm or aperture of a camera that adjusts the amount of light that gets to the film of the eye, called the retina.

Our eyes don't glow in the dark, because we have a layer of dark pigment behind our retina that absorbs or soaks up light. Very little light reflects back out of the eye. Many animals, including cats and deer, have a reflective layer of cells behind the retina, called the *tapetum lucidum*, which in Latin means "luminous carpet."

So cats, deer, and many nocturnal animals have two chances to see light. The first is when light goes into the eye; the second is as it reflects back out. This makes their vision far more sensitive than ours but somewhat blurry. They see better in the dark, but they can't see fine detail. When you and I see an animal's eyes glowing in the dark, it is because we are seeing some of the reflected light bouncing back from that reflective layer of cells.

By the way, you may have noticed that a cat's pupil is slit-shaped. The cat has to be able to see well in dark but also needs to 'stop down' or block out bright daylight glare. Our human round pupil eye can't close down as much as a cat's slit-shaped pupil. So the cat is able to block more light from going into the eye.

Try this simple light experiment. Make a light trap that is blacker than black. Find a half gallon ice cream container. The inside of most ice cream containers is white in color.

Cut a small (about 1/4 inch diameter) hole in the center of the lid. Put the lid on the box and look into the hole. Even though the interior of the box is white, what you see inside the hole appears perfectly black.

What is going on here? When the light enters the hole, it bounces around many times. With each bounce, some light is absorbed by the inside surface. After so many bounces, hardly any light is left to come out of the hole. The pupil of our eye looks black for the same reason.

## Q19: What would happen if you put a DNA sample from a human into another creature?

If we're talking about a cross between a human and a Holstein cow, well, that's not going to happen. But in fact, animal-human hybrid work has been going on for a number of years in labs all over the world. Thousands of animals contain human cells or DNA. Most of these are mice with a single gene sequence of human origin.

There are mice with human-like livers that allow scientists to study the effects of drugs. Pig liver cells have been used experimentally to cleanse the blood of people with liver failure, hoping to keep them alive until a donor can be found.

Some lab monkeys carry a human form of the Huntington's disease gene that permits scientists to investigate the development of the disease. A fatal hereditary disease, Huntington's disease destroys areas of the brain used for intellect, emotions, and movement.

There are sheep and pigs with bits of human organs growing inside them. The goal is that these animals will grow organs that can be used by humans.

Pig, cow, and dog heart valves have been used to replace faulty valves in humans for a number of years. There is hope that pig pancreas cells can be used for diabetes treatment. Fetal pig neurons have been implanted into the brains of people with Parkinson's disease.

Parkinson's disease is caused by brain cells that die and cause changes in feelings and motion. Parkinson's disease is often characterized by shaking and tremors of the limbs, poor posture, and loss of balance.

DNA from humans is inserted into bacteria to re-create the insulin gene, and the insulin is used for many diabetic patients nationwide. This is true of other important therapeutic molecules as well.

The goal of all this "recombinant DNA technology" research is to save lives and to study drugs and diseases. Some recent research has been truly exciting. Scientists are doing to brain cells what they have previously done with liver and kidney cells. There are now humanized mice with Alzheimer's symptoms to help find an answer to the neurological disorders which kills almost two million people worldwide each year.

Recombinant DNA technology is not the same as whole body cloning. Cloning is the process of creating an identical copy of an organism. Dolly, the sheep, was cloned in Scotland in 1996 as an exact copy of her mother. No ram was involved. A cell was taken from Dolly's biological mother and transferred into the egg of a female sheep. The egg was implanted into the surrogate mother, where it grew into a fetus and eventually into an identical baby copy of the original animal. Dolly, the baby, lived for six years.

Dolly was controversial, and cloning is not simple. The success rate is terrible. Dolly was born after 277 eggs were used to create 29 embryos, which produced three lambs, of which only one lived.

There is talk about bringing back extinct species by cloning dead specimens and growing them in the wombs of similar animals. The woolly mammoth has been extinct since 1700 B.C., but the DNA of these creatures has been preserved fairly intact in the frozen ice of the Russian tundra. Could woolly mammoth DNA be injected into the egg of a modern elephant?

This DNA transfer and cloning have raised serious moral and ethical issues. Should we be tampering with Mother Nature? What are the risks and benefits? Is our science ahead of our rules and regulations in this area?

# Chapter Three

# The Science of
# Food and Drink

Pellagra is common in people who have a lot of corn and little else in their diet. Pellagra can occur if the body does not absorb niacin or tryptophan. It can develop after gastrointestinal diseases or with alcoholism. Symptoms include delusional thinking, mental confusion, diarrhea, and scaly skin sores. In 1901 the English biochemist Frederick G. Hopkins isolated tryptophan from casein, the major protein found in milk. That's why drinking a glass of warm milk before going to bed is said to induce sleep.

We tend to think of turkey and tryptophan as being tied together. But tryptophan is also found abundantly in chocolate, milk, yogurt, cottage cheese, eggs, bananas, peanuts, and fish.

## Q22: *How can you tell a raw egg from a hard-boiled egg?*

Use Newton's First Law of Motion, which refers to inertia. An object in motion wants to stay in motion and an object at rest wants to stay at rest.

Separately spin a hard-boiled and a raw egg on a horizontal surface.

The hard-boiled egg will spin easily. It is solid all the way to the center. Every part of the egg spins together. Once you have the hard-boiled egg spinning, grasp it quickly and then let go of it. The boiled egg will stop spinning.

The raw egg is hard to get spinning. The inside is liquid. You spin the shell, but the yolk and white want to stay at rest. Once you get the egg spinning, grasp it quickly to stop it momentarily. The inside portions continue to spin. When you let go, the egg starts spinning again because the contents inside imparts frictional forces to the shell and pulls it along.

Try this simple egg science experiment. Do the raw egg and hard-boiled egg test described above. Note that the hard-boiled egg will stand up on one end when it is rapidly spinning. The mass of a rapidly spinning object wants to go as close to the spin axis as possible. The spinning egg becomes dynamically stable. An egg standing on one end has a smaller radius around its axis of spin compared to an egg on its side. Therefore, the spinning lifts the egg onto one end and raises its center of gravity.

### Q23: How do they make freeze-dried coffee?

. . . . . . . . . . . . . . . . . . . . . . . . . . . . . . . . .

The basic principle of freeze-drying is the removal of water by sublimation. You can experience freeze drying in your own freezer or freezer compartment of your refrigerator. Take a thin slice of apple and put it in the freezer without any wrapper or covering. It will freeze and then it will start to dry out

The water sublimates out of the apple, going straight from solid ice to water vapor. The liquid state of matter has been skipped. After some time, the apple will contain no water. It has been freeze-dried. This process will take days or weeks. To speed up the process, the apple slice could be put in a vacuum. Once freeze-dried, the apple slice can be stored for many years without spoiling. When a person wants to eat the apple slice, all they need is some hot water to restore the original taste and texture.

In the case of freeze-dried coffee, suppliers make 2,000-pound batches of extremely strong brew and then freeze it into blocks of solid ice-coffee. Then they pulverize the blocks into fine granules and put them in a vacuum chamber. The water molecules are sucked right out of the granules, ice turning to vapor, leaving dried granules of coffee behind.

Freeze-drying reduces the weight of a substance. Some fruits are 80 to 90 percent water. Campers, hikers, and the military are big time users of freeze-dried products. NASA has used freeze-dried foods for fifty years in the cramped quarters of spacecraft. Astronauts' food is usually freeze-dried until they add water from their fuel cells. Fuel cells mix oxygen and hydrogen to produce electricity. One of the by-products of a fuel cell is extremely pure water.

Freeze-drying is used on flowers at weddings. It makes them last longer, sometimes longer than the marriage! Freeze-drying can also be used to restore water-damaged manuscripts and documents.

Freeze-dried coffee and other foodstuffs that use a strong vacuum came out of research done during WWII. The military wanted a way to manufacture and ship blood plasma, penicillin, and other antibiotics. One of the first successful uses of this technology was concentrated orange juice powder. The company that did military work with orange juice later changed its name to Minute Maid.

## Q24: Why is milk white?

Milk contains casein, a protein rich in calcium. Casein surrounds the fat globules that are in milk. When light waves hit the molecules that make up casein, cream, and fat, they bounce off or reflect in every direction. The globules act as mirrors. The process is known as scattering.

So the whiteness is due to the scattering of light by the colloidal particles of the milk emulsion. All wavelengths or colors of light are scattered (reflected) by the same amount. And whenever an object reflects all colors equally, the result is white.

The more cream (fat globules) found in milk, the whiter it appears. The 2 percent milk in the blue cap carton and 1 percent milk in the pink cap carton appear more bluish because the milk contains less cream.

Milk is a healthy drink, providing calcium for bones and teeth and Vitamin D for bones. Milk also contains Vitamin B12 and magnesium.

A lack of Vitamin B12 affects every part of the nervous system. Magnesium is needed for normal heart rhythm, the immune system, and muscle control.

Milk comes from a cow's udder at a temperature of about 101 degrees Fahrenheit. Milk is then quickly cooled to 40 degrees. If left unprocessed, the less dense cream will float to the top of the container, and the more dense water, or whey, will sink to the bottom. Hence the expression "the cream rises to the top."

The milk we buy in the store is homogenized. The cow's milk is run through tiny tubes that break up the fat globules into tinier pieces so that they remain suspended in the milk.

Pasteurization, the heating of the milk, is also a standard practice. Heating the milk kills bacteria making the milk safer to drink.

Here is my favorite milk joke:

Lady: "I want 54 quarts of milk."

Store Clerk: "You want 54 quarts of milk. Why so much?"

Lady: "I want to take a milk bath."

Store clerk: "Do you want it pasteurized?"

Lady: "No, just up to my chin."

## Q25: Is it better to drain the water, or keep the water around ice cubes, if you're trying to keep something cold in a cooler?

• • • • • • • • • • • • • • • • • • • • • • • • • • • • • • • • • • • • • • • • • • • • • • • •

This is an excellent question for people going on picnics, tailgate parties, or long car trips. Keep the water in the ice chest. There is no need to drain the water from recently melted ice unless you have something in the cooler that could become soggy.

The science says this: A can of pop, or perhaps a stronger beverage, will have one of three things in contact with it; air, water, or ice. More than likely, a combination of all three will touch the can.

Ice will be at a temperature of 32 degree Fahrenheit. Ice right out of the freezer can be colder than 32, but after a few minutes in the ice chest, it's going to be 32 and no colder. At 32 degrees, the ice melts and turns to water. The water resulting from the melted ice will also be extremely close to 32.

So two out of three things in contact with the soda can will be at a temperature of 32 degrees. The air in the cooler is most likely to be several degrees above 32. And it will become much higher than 32 degrees if people keep opening the cooler to get a "cold one." So you can see that you're better off not draining the water out of the cooler. If you drain the water, you would have warmer air in contact with the beverage can rather than the colder water.

There are several other things you can do to maximize the useful time of a cooler. Store the cooler in a cool place for several hours before using it. Cool down the food and beverages that will go into the cooler. Use large cubes, not small cubes. Large cubes have less total surface area compared to small cubes, so they melt more slowly. Large cubes kept above the beverages is a good bet. The water melted from the large cubes will drain among the cans of beverages. The newly melted ice at 32 degrees is now cold water close to 32 degrees. Keep the lid closed as much as possible. Maintain the cooler in a shaded area, not in direct sunlight. You can also use re-freezable ice substitutes. They don't shed any water, but cool the air above the beverages.

Igloo, largest manufacturer of coolers in the United States, advertises a "5-day cooler." To test the ice chest, they put in a fixed amount of ice in the cooler and then place the cooler in a 90-degree oven to simulate warm outdoor conditions. The temperature and time are logged until all the ice is melted and water inside reaches 39 degrees. They put a big "5 days" on their label. Keep in mind that Igloo keeps the lid closed during the test.

## Q26: Why don't microwaves leak out through the holes in the microwave oven door?

Microwaves don't leak out because the holes are too small. If we could actually see microwaves they would look much like water waves that have crests and troughs. The waves that cook our food in a microwave oven are about five inches (12.5 centimeters) long. The holes in the mesh screen of the microwave oven door are quite small, so the waves "see" it as a solid sheet of metal.

Visible light waves are tiny waves that get through the holes so you and I can see what's cooking. The holes are small for microwaves but they are huge for light. As a matter of fact, the holes in the mesh screen door are about a hundred times smaller than the microwaves that might try to get out.

Satellite dish antennas are often "mesh-like" rather than solid. The holes allow air to get through to cut down on wind resistance, but the holes are almost invisible as far as television signals are concerned. Waterproof Gore-Tex materials are based on the same idea. The holes in the fabric allow air to pass through. But the holes are far too small for water molecules to pass through. We say that the Gore-Tex clothing is breathable.

To illustrate the relationship between hole size and area, try to answer these two questions. You have a circle that is 1 inch across (diameter). If you double the diameter, how much do you increase the area of the circle? If you make the circle into a sphere, (a three-dimensional circle), how much do you increase the volume?

Answer: The area will be four times greater and the volume will be eight times as much. The area is proportional to the square of the radius. The volume is proportional to the cube of the radius.

## Q27: How can shaking and opening a bottle of cold soft drink make it suddenly freeze?

Soft drinks, or carbonated beverages, contain carbon dioxide gas under pressure. It is this carbon dioxide that gives the pop its fizz. Much of that carbon dioxide is dissolved in the soda when the can is pressurized.

Suppose you leave a bottle or can of soda outside in cold weather until the temperature of the pop is close to freezing. That would be near 32 Fahrenheit or 0 Centigrade (Celsius). So the temperature would not have to drop much further for the soda to freeze.

Now suppose you shake the can. When you open the can or bottle, the pressure inside is released and the gas expands. When a compressed gas expands, it cools down. In some cases, the temperature drops quite a bit. That lost heat has to come from somewhere. And that somewhere is the contents of the bottle or can. The soda loses heat, enough to drop its temperature below the freezing point.

Let's take the opposite case. When gases are compressed, they heat up. That's why the coils on the back of the refrigerator get hot. Those coils contain compressed gas that will later be condensing into a liquid. When a liquid evaporates, going from a liquid state to a gas state, it absorbs heat in the process. That heat comes from the contents of the fridge.

That gas has to be compressed again and it takes work to do it. The compressor is run by a motor, and that is what we pay for when we operate a refrigerator or freezer. Air conditioning works on the same principle.

Evaporation is a cooling process. If you pour a bit of rubbing alcohol on your skin, it feels cool. The alcohol is evaporating rapidly, and absorbs heat. That heat comes from the skin, making us feel cool.

Natural gas is purified by removing water, oil, mud, and other gases. Then it is cooled down to -260 degrees Fahrenheit. It turns into a liquid. Condensing into a liquid decreases the volume of natural gas by 600 times, making it possible to ship liquefied natural gas (LNG) all over the world.

Condensation means going from a gas state to a liquid state. Condensation is a warming process. A quite subtle example of condensation being a warming process takes place in the winter. Let's say the temperature is about 20 degrees Fahrenheit, and it starts to snow. After two or three hours of snow, the temperature will rise to about 22 or 23 degrees Fahrenheit. It is such a small rise in temperature that most people don't notice it. Snowing is condensation, followed by freezing, and that condensation warms the atmosphere by a couple of degrees.

Larry Scheckel

## Q28: Why does an egg solidify when it is heated instead of turning into a gas?

A very good observation! When solid material, such as a metal, is heated, it usually turns to a liquid then a gas as it goes through each state of matter. The same, but opposite sequence, occurs when matter cools. The progression is from gas, to liquid, and then to a solid.

When a solid such as ice is heated, enough heat is transferred to the molecules to allow them to break the chemical bonds that hold them in a solid crystalline state. When these molecules can move around and slide over each other, we call it liquid water. Similarly, when liquid water is heated sufficiently, the molecules vibrate so violently, they escape the surface and enter into a vapor state.

But not all phase changes between a solid and a liquid are strictly about melting and cooling. Examples include congealing scrambled eggs and polymerizing plastics. The egg is one of those oddities. An egg is made of proteins that consist of long-chained molecules twisted but held in a roughly spherical shape by chemical bonds. As the egg is heated, these bonds break. The molecules unravel and bond with other molecules to form a network that traps water and turns the egg into a solid.

Continual heating of the egg causes the formation of more covalent bonds between neighbors, and the egg becomes less watery and more solid. These strong stable bonds are termed disulfide bridges. This cross-linking makes the chains form networks so the egg hardens.

By the way, eggs are very good for us humans. Those albumen proteins are most valuable. The egg yolk and egg whites contain all eight essential amino acids. Eggs are a significant source of iron, riboflavin, folate, and vitamins B12, D, and E. The fact that eggs have Vitamin D stands out because they are one of few foods that contain this particular vitamin.

One large egg has about 180 mg of cholesterol, all of it found in the yolk. So the recommendation is that people with high levels of the LDL cholesterol (that's the bad one) should limit their consumption of eggs. There are now cholesterol-free egg substitutes on the market. They're made from egg whites.

# Chapter Four

# Remarkable People in Science

## Q29: *What is highest recorded human IQ?*

M arilyn vos Savant became famous when the Guinness Book of World Records listed her from 1986-1989 under the category "Highest IQ" with a score of 190. However, Guinness discontinued that designation in 1990, saying that IQ tests are not reliable enough to choose a single world record holder.

Marilyn vos Savant, born in 1946, is a regular columnist for Parade Magazine, the Sunday supplement found in hundreds of newspapers. She has written the column since 1986 and is married to Dr. Robert Jarvik, inventor of the artificial heart. Her column answers questions from readers and solves puzzles.

IQ stands for Intelligence Quotient. It is a score that reportedly tells one how bright a person is compared to other people. The average IQ is 100. Scores above 100 indicate a higher IQ and below 100 is a lower IQ. Half the population has scores between 90 and 110.

Traditionally, there have been two tests that measure IQ, the Stanford-Binet (version 5) and the Wechsler Intelligence Test for Children. Intelligence tests do not measure how much a person knows. They measure how good a person is at figuring out things, that is, the person's reasoning skills.

Many high school students take the American College Testing (ACT) test or the SAT, the Scholastic Aptitude Test. They are closely related to intelligence tests and are about as good as high school grades in predicting college success, especially during the first year. Beyond freshman year, success in college depends mostly on an individual's drive and determination to set and accomplish goals that are important.

Who does have the highest IQ? Korean Kim Ung-Yong, born in 1962, began speaking at four months of age, read four languages by his second birthday, and did calculus at age three. He has a verified IQ of 210 and worked at NASA for four years in the mid 1970's. Israeli Prime Minister Benjamin Netanyahu had an IQ measured at 180. Physicist Steven Hawking comes in at 160, and actress Sharon Stone has an IQ of 154.

It's important to remember what IQ does not measure. It does not measure creativity, empathy, kindness, integrity, character, attitude, curiosity, motivation, or good judgment. Even Marilyn vos Savant claims that "intelligence involves many factors, and attempts to measure it are useless."

My wife, Ann, and I recently returned from a two-week tour of Germany. One of the places we visited was the palatial villa in a Berlin suburb where the Wannsee Conference was held on January 20, 1942. Reinhard Heydrich, who chaired the Wannsee Conference, was tasked with the "final solution to the Jewish question," a plan having the full approval of Adolf Hitler. Of the fifteen members, nine had earned a doctorate or PhD, including Adolf Eichmann. So being smart does not always equate to being a good human being.

The Mensa Society is open to people whose intelligence is in the upper two percent of the general population. To be a member you must do well on an approved intelligence test that is properly administered and supervised. Then Mensa will ask you to join. No Scheckel has ever been asked to join!

## Q30: Who was the greatest scientist of all time?

It comes down to a matter of opinion. It's like asking "Who was the greatest baseball player or best quarterback of all time?" or "Who was the greatest president in the history of the United States?"

There are probably a dozen or more scientists that would make anyone's Top Twenty list. They would have to include

Albert Einstein, Isaac Newton, Charles Darwin, Niels Bohr, Max Planck, Galileo, Nikola Tesla, Michael Faraday, Johannes Kepler, Leonardo da Vinci, Archimedes, and Aristotle.

My pick is Isaac Newton. Some would say Einstein. He seems to be the best known. But even Einstein admitted that much of his work would have been impossible without the discoveries of Isaac Newton. Newton was born in England in 1642, the same year Galileo died. His father died three months before he was born. Newton was raised by his grandmother until age eight. His mother remarried a wealthy landowner. Then the rich guy died. Newton was a failure at farming so he attended Trinity College, graduating with a Master's degree at age 23.

The plague swept through England from 1665 to 1668, and all the universities were closed. So Newton went home to his inherited estates at Woolsthorpe. In those three years, Newton's genius blossomed. He discovered the laws of motion and universal gravitation, the foundation of modern physics. He made breakthroughs in the understanding of light, color, and optics. He proved that light is made up of seven colors of the rainbow. He invented the branch of mathematics known as calculus. In 1668, Newton invented the reflecting telescope, which overcame the difficulties of blurring (chromatic aberration) caused by using Galileo's refracting telescope. At the urging of a friend, Robert Halley, Newton published a book called the *Principia* in 1687. It is to this day considered to be the greatest single written work in the history of science. Elected to the Royal Society, knighted by Queen Anne, made Master of the Royal Mint, he never married. He became embroiled in a bitter argument with Gottfried Leibniz over who invented the calculus. (Newton invented it first, but published it second).

Newton himself considered his study of the Bible his most important work. He spent a lot of time trying to find hidden passages, secret embedded codes, and Bible prophecies. He had his faults. Newton was a poor lecturer, dabbled in alchemy, and was mean-spirited, quarrelsome, and vindictive.

As a testament to his life's importance, the pallbearers at his funeral included the Lord High Chancellor, two dukes, three earls, and a host of dignitaries from the Mint and Royal Society.

After Newton's death, his body was found to contain massive amounts of mercury. The accumulation of mercury was probably due to his work in alchemy. Because mercury is a neurotoxin, this gradual poisoning no doubt contributed to Newton's personality quirks in later life.

## Q31: *Who invented the computer?*

Computers developed from mechanical calculating machines. One of the earliest mechanical machines, still used today, is the abacus, a wooden frame with parallel rods on which beads are strung.

Blaise Pascal, while still a teenager, invented a simple mechanism for adding and subtracting in 1642. In the mid 1850's, Charles Babbage conceived the idea of a machine that would undertake any kind of calculation. The machine would be driven by steam, and the entire program of operations would be stored on a punched tape. Babbage's "analytical engine" was never built, but his ideas are used in modern computers. Babbage enjoys the title of "the father of the computer."

Punched cards were developed early as a way of programming or giving instructions to a machine. Their first use was to direct automated pattern weaving on a loom. Cards with holes directed threads on the loom, with wire hooks passing through the holes to grab and pull specific colored threads to be woven into the cloth. Punched cards were also used in the 1890 United States Census. Metal pins in the machine's reader passed through holes punched in the card, momentarily closing an electric circuit. The resulting pulses advanced counters assigned to details, such as income and family size.

The company that developed this tabulated machine became IBM in 1924. Their 80-column, 7.375 by 3.25-inch card became the standard of the industry. IBM printed, "Do not fold, spindle, or mutilate" on each card.

The earliest programmable electronic computer was the brainchild of Alan Turing, built by Newman and Flowers in 1943 and called "Colossus." With 1500 vacuum tubes, Colossus frequently broke down, but using it, the British were able to break the code generated by the German "Enigma" machines.

Right after WWII, the United States made a mammoth computer using vacuum tubes and drum memories, called ENIAC. It had over 17,000 vacuum tubes, weighed 30 tons, measured a hundred feet long, eight feet high, and three feet deep, and used over 15 kilowatts of power. Los Alamos labs used an ENIAC to develop the hydrogen bomb in the early 1950's.

Invented in 1948, the transistor greatly reduced the size, complexity, and power requirements of electronics, and increased the speed at the same time. By the early 1960's, silicon chips packed thousands of transistors and circuit components onto a wafer.

There is plenty of new computer technology on the way. Gallium arsenide has greatly increased switching speed. Organic polymers, used for liquid crystal panels and other flat screen displays, have vast potential. Optical chips that push around light instead of electrons have shown promise.

So to answer the question, "Who invented the computer?" an honest answer would be "a whole bunch of people." Computers have involved a steady progression of knowledge, research, advancing technology, and material development by a host of smart and motivated people.

## Q32: *How many women have won the Nobel Prize?*

The Nobel Prizes in Chemistry, Physics, Physiology/ Medicine, Literature, and Economic Science are awarded annually in Stockholm by the Royal Swedish Academy of Science. The more famous Nobel Peace Prize is awarded annually in Oslo, Norway on December 10, the anniversary of Nobel's death. The King and Queen of Norway attend.

Four women have earned the Nobel Prize in Chemistry. The best known is Marie Curie, in 1911, for the separation of pure radium. Her daughter won the Chemistry Prize in 1935 for the discovery of artificial radioactivity.

Two women won the Nobel Prize in Physics. Marie Curie won her second prize in 1903 for the discovery of radioactivity. The other winner was Maria Goeppert Mayer in 1963, for her work on how the atomic nucleus works.

Ten women have earned the Nobel Prize in the field of Physiology and Medicine. Best known are Rosalyn Yalow (1977) for work in radioisotope tracing and Barbara McClintock (1983) for her studies of corn genetics.

Pearl Buck is one of twelve women awarded the Nobel Prize in Literature. Her 1938 Nobel Prize cited her "rich and truly epic description of peasant life in China." Her best-known book is "The Good Earth." which also won the Pulitzer Prize.

The first and only woman to win the Nobel Prize in Economic Sciences is Elinor Ostrom (2009) "for her analysis of how common property could be managed by groups using [the commons]."

Fifteen women have won the Nobel Peace Prize. The most recognized include Jane Addams (1931), founder of Hull House in Chicago, and Mother Teresa (1979), a native Albanian nun who founded missions for the poor in India, starting in Calcutta.

History now recognizes one woman who really got cheated out of a Nobel Prize: Lise Meitner. Born in Austria in 1878, Meitner was half of the team that discovered nuclear fission. Meitner and Otto Hahn worked together at the Kaiser Wilhelm Institute in Berlin, Germany. When Hitler came to power in 1933, Lise Meitner, born of Jewish parents, was protected by her Austrian citizenship. But after the *Anschluss*, the annexation of Austria into the Third Reich in March, 1938, Meitner's situation became desperate. She made a daring undercover escape to the Netherlands, then traveled to neutral Sweden.

Lise Meitner corresponded with Otto Hahn and the two met in Copenhagen in November, 1938. They planned to carry out a new round of experiments on bombarding uranium with neutrons, but Meitner could not go back to Nazi Germany, so the experiment was carried out by Otto Hahn and Fritz Strassmann.

It was Lise Meitner and her nephew Otto Frisch who correctly interpreted the result of the experiment. Hahn and Strassman had detected the element barium after bombarding uranium with neutrons. Meitner and Frisch explained the physics of how uranium could be split into two smaller atoms. Now the whole world knew that "fission" of the uranium atom was possible, with a tremendous release of power. Because the reaction also released several neutrons, a chain reaction could lead to nuclear power or an atomic bomb.

Otto Hahn was awarded the Nobel Prize in 1944. Missing from the ceremony was Lise Meitner. In 1964, *Physics Today* concluded that "personal negative opinions led to the exclusion of a deserving scientist" from the Nobel Prize. Element 109, "Meitnerium," is named in Lise Meitner's honor.

## Q33: Did Thomas Jefferson ever invent anything?
. . . . . . . . . . . . . . . . . . . . . . . . . . . . . . . . . . . . .

The third president of the United States was a busy and creative genius. Jefferson was an esteemed politician, statesman, farmer, writer, educator, architect, and inventor. He loved making things. "Nature intended me for the tranquil pursuits of science, by rendering them my supreme delight," he wrote.

A steward of the soil, Jefferson made a huge improvement on the moldboard of the plow. The wooden plowshares of the time dug down only two or three inches into the soil. Jefferson's improvement of the Dutch moldboard, based on a mathematical design, dug down six inches. The plow also turned the soil over better, which helped prevent erosion. Jefferson never patented the improvements he made to the plow, but later steel plows were based on his design.

While serving as George Washington's Secretary of State from 1790 to 1793, Jefferson needed a means of secretly communicating with his colleagues. Correspondence was frequently intercepted by foreign governments and read. Jefferson devised a wheel cipher with 26 cylindrical wooden pieces that looked like large Oreo cookies threaded onto an iron rod. The letters of the alphabet were written in random order around the edge of each wheel. Turning these wheels, words could be scrambled and unscrambled. Governments used variations of this code device all the way up to WWII.

Jefferson devised a rotating stand which held 5 books. The book rests could be folded to make a box attached to a base. Libraries worldwide have copied this ingenious book stand.

Jefferson's Great Clock can be seen at Monticello, Virginia. It's powered by cannonballs left over from the Revolutionary War. The cannonball weights hang from both sides of the doorway. The days of the week can be read from markings on the wall.

The great clock face can be seen from both inside and outside the house.

To service the Great Clock, Jefferson devised a folding ladder that could also be used to prune trees. This kind of ladder is still used in many libraries to reach high book shelves.

John Isaac Hawkins made a "polygraph" machine consisting of two connecting pens that moved synchronously to produce an exact and immediate copy of anything he wrote. Jefferson acquired one of the machines in 1804 and used it until his death in 1826. He had one installed in what is now called the White House. He placed another in his Monticello home. Jefferson made several improvements on the machine. (The term "polygraph" is used today to mean lie detector. Hawkins and Jefferson machines would now be called pantographs).

The gifted visionary made a mechanical dumb waiter which permitted servants to send wine bottles up from the cellar. He also produced a sundial shaped like a globe. The original was lost but reproductions exist, based on his 1816 letter to architect Benjamin Henry Latrobe.

In 1804, Jefferson had glass doors installed between the hall and parlor in his home. A mechanism with two wheels joined by a chain in a figure eight arrangement and hidden under the floor allowed both doors to move when one was opened or closed. Jefferson also invented the swivel chair, a pedometer, and a hemp-treating machine.

Thomas Jefferson viewed patents as monopolies. He could have made a bundle on his dumbwaiter, great clock, hideaway bed, pedometer, copying machine, swivel chair, macaroni extruding device, sundial, revolving bookstand, and improved plow moldboard.

Thomas Jefferson served two terms as President of the United States, from 1801 to 1809. He doubled the size of our country with the Louisiana Purchase in 1803-1804. Jefferson got his head sculptured on Mt. Rushmore and his mug on the two-dollar bill.

Larry Scheckel

## Q34: What patents were issued to famous Americans who were not inventors?

On May 22, 1849, twelve years before he became president, Abraham Lincoln was granted a patent for a device to help steamboats pass over shoals and sand bars. It was the only patent ever issued to a United States president.

The device had a set of adjustable buoyancy chambers, made from metal and waterproof cloth, attached to the ship's side below the waterline. Bellows would fill the chambers with air to float the vessel upward and over the obstruction or sandbar.

Lincoln had a fascination with tools and mechanical things. He gave lectures on inventions and discoveries, once stating that "man is not the only animal who labors, but the only one who improves his workmanship."

Lincoln traveled extensively, twice taking a flatboat from Indiana and Ohio all the way down to New Orleans. He combined a curious mind with love of tools and machinery and was constantly looking to improve things. The story goes that when Lincoln was returning home to Illinois in 1848 from a session in Congress, his boat became stranded on a sand bar. The crew and passengers eventually freed the boat by forcing empty barrels and casks under the boat until the boat was lifted high enough to free it. When Lincoln got back to Illinois, he made a scale model of his intended invention. The device was never used or even tested, but his scale model is on display at the Smithsonian Institution in Washington, D.C.

The author Mark Twain was awarded three patents. His 1871 patent was for suspenders. Actually, it was for an adjustable elastic strap with a clasp that holds "vests, pantaloons, or other garments requiring straps." It was supposed to tighten shirts at the waist, taking the place of suspenders. Today that invention is used on the brassiere.

Twain's 1873 patent was his Self-Pasting Scrapbook. The leaves of the book are "entirely covered with mucilage or other adhesive substance." He went on to say that "one only has to moisten the leaf, place a piece to be pasted and it will stick to the leaf."

His third invention in 1885 was an educational memory game to help people recall historical dates. His Memory Builder game was a result of a version he developed to teach his own children the history of England's monarchs.

Mark Twain claimed the scrapbook patent made him $50,000 compared to his lifetime writing earnings of $200,000. He was a better writer than money manager. Twain was fascinated by technology and financially backed a bunch of losers, which led him to bankruptcy. He was forced to go on a world-wide lecture tour to pay off his debts.

Unlike Thomas Jefferson, Mark Twain, Father of American Literature, could not afford to give his inventions away.

### Q35: Why did Benjamin Franklin fly a kite during a thunderstorm?

B en Franklin's kite experiment is firmly fixed in American legend and lore. Franklin proved that lightning is a discharge of static electricity. He was lucky he did not get killed.

Several experimenters in France were electrocuted when they tried to repeat Franklin's feat.

What did Franklin do? In June, 1752, the 48-year-old Ben Franklin and his 21-year-old son, William, devised a kite from a large silk handkerchief and two cross-sticks. To the top of the kite, they affixed a very sharp wire that stuck about one foot above the kite. The other end of the thin wire was attached to the kite string twine. To the other end of the twine, the one on the ground, they fastened a key. From the junction of the twine and key, Franklin tied a smaller dry silk handkerchief. A thin metal wire was attached to the key and the other end inserted into a Leyden jar, a glass jar used to store electricity.

The pair of experimenters found a shed in a field outside of Philadelphia. In Franklin's own words, "Dreading the ridicule which too commonly attends unsuccessful attempts in science," they wanted a place that was isolated from the public. They waited a considerable time, almost giving up, for the dark clouds of an approaching thunderstorm to pass above them. Up went the kite. They dashed inside the shed to keep that silk handkerchief dry. The rain wetted the kite and twine so as to conduct the electricity freely. Franklin held the dry handkerchief in one hand and brought the knuckles from his free hand up to the key. That is when he received a shock.

Franklin showed that lightning is of the equivalent nature as static electricity; both caused by friction. Scientists at the time were familiar with the static electricity obtained "by rubbing a glass globe or tube with silk."

Franklin was the first to describe electricity as a "common element" which he called "electric fire," and the first to assert that electricity was fluid, like a liquid. Before Franklin's time, electricity was thought of as two opposing forces.

Franklin's work became the basis of the single fluid theory that electricity flows from a body with a negative charge, which we now know means an excess of electrons, to a positive body that has a deficiency of electrons. That flow business can get a bit complicated, because some electrical engineers use "conventional current flow" (positive to negative) and many people use "electron flow" (negative to positive).

Franklin never did publish his account of the famous kite experiment. Franklin wrote a description of his research to his good friend, Joseph Priestly, who published the story some 15 years after it happened. Priestly was a distinguished theologian, political theorist, and scientist (natural philosopher).

Ben Franklin is known for his leadership during the Revolutionary War, his invention of the Franklin stove, bifocals, glass harmonica, and lightning rods. He established fire departments and library systems. But Franklin was also a first-rate scientist, especially in the area of electricity. In honor of his accomplishments, Franklin gets his face on the hundred-dollar bill.

These terms and words came about because of Ben Franklin: battery, conductor, plus, minus, positive, negative, armature, charge, and condenser.

### Q36: Who was the only person to win the Nobel Prize in Physics twice?

. . . . . . . . . . . . . . . . . . . . . . . . . . . . . . . . . . . . . . . . . . . . . . . .

John Bardeen (1908-1991) is the only person to have won the Nobel Prize in Physics twice. His first Nobel Prize was in 1956 for the invention of the transistor. He shared the Nobel Prize with William Shockley and Walter Brattain.

The second Nobel Prize was awarded in 1972 for the theory of superconductivity. He shared that prize with Leon Cooper and John Schrieffer.

John Bardeen has a strong Wisconsin connection. He grew up in Madison, Wisconsin. His father was a doctor and professor at the UW-Madison. His mother died when he was twelve years old. His father remarried a year later. Young Bardeen skipped three grades, going from third grade into seventh grade at the University High School in Madison.

Bardeen earned his master's degree in electrical engineering in 1929, and his Ph.D. in math from Princeton University in 1936. He worked as a geophysicist for Gulf Oil. During WWII, Bardeen was a government employee for the Naval Ordinance Lab in the field of submarine warfare.

Hired by Bell Labs in New Jersey after the war, Bardeen worked on the problem of a replacement for vacuum tubes used in electronic equipment. Vacuum tubes were heavy, fragile, bulky, and power hungry. They needed ventilation and burned out after a few years. The Bell Lab team succeeded in December, 1947, when the device that would change electronics forever, the transistor, was born. A solid-state device made of silicon or germanium, it could switch and amplify signals. It paved the way for radio, calculators, and computers. America could never have gone to the moon without the transistor and its subsequent integrated circuit (computer chip). The transistor changed the life of every American.

Later, working at the University of Illinois, at Champaign-Urbana, John Bardeen and his team pioneered research on superconductivity, which eventually led to MRI machines used in hospitals. Later the team worked on light-emitting diodes. Bardeen was a professor at the University of Illinois for 40 years.

Superconductivity, the process where a conductor loses all resistance to electron flow, eluded the most famous scientists of the 1900s, including Albert Einstein, Niels Bohr, Werner Heisenberg, and Richard Feynman.

John Bardeen led a quiet, unassuming life. His greatest joy was taking his family on picnics, barbecuing for neighbors, and playing golf. On the outside, he did not appear to be the genius that he was.

John Bardeen married biologist Jane Maxwell in 1938. Their two sons are physicists like their father, and their only daughter is a geologist.

In 1956, when Bardeen was award the Nobel Prize in Stockholm, Sweden, King Gustav chastised him for bringing only one of his children. Bardeen replied that next time he would bring all three. In 1972, all five Bardeens attended the Nobel Prize ceremony. John and Jane Bardeen are buried in Forest Hill Cemetery in Madison, Wisconsin.

## Q37: *What did Louis Pasteur do?*
. . . . . . . . . . . . . . . . . . . . . . . . . . . . .

Louis Pasteur (1822-1895) was a French microbiologist and chemist best known for the principle of pasteurization, fermentation, and vaccination. Hailed today as a hero and a giant in scientific accomplishments, Pasteur was initially considered a quack by the medical people of Paris.

Pasteur and his wife, Marie, had five children, but three died of typhoid at early ages. These personal losses motivated Pasteur to find a cure for infectious diseases.

Pasteur discovered microscopic organisms in sour wine. He found that these organisms could be killed by heating. In 1862, Pasteur extended this method to protecting milk. His technique of treating milk to halt bacterial contamination is now known as pasteurization.

Pasteur found that fermentation was due to the growth of micro-organisms, and not to "spontaneous generation," or the appearance of life from non-living matter. Tiny organisms occur naturally in the environment, and do not appear out of nowhere. Pasteur reasoned that if organisms could contaminate beverages such as wine and milk, then such organisms might also infect animals and humans, thus causing diseases. This was a radical idea. The prevalent thinking at that time was that organisms were the result of a disease, not the cause of a disease.

Work on chicken cholera led Pasteur to hit upon the idea of immunity. Weakened bacteria caused the chickens to become immune to the disease. The concept of a weak form of a disease preventing a deadly version was not new. Edward Jenner, in 1796, had demonstrated that cowpox vaccination gave immunity to smallpox.

Pasteur's breakthrough came when he discovered the weakened form could be generated artificially, so that a naturally weakened form did not have to be found. He applied the immunization theory to anthrax, which affected cattle, and was granted a patent on the production of an anthrax vaccine. Pasteur gave these manufactured weakened forms the name "vaccine" in honor of Jenner.

Pasteur's work led to vaccines for smallpox, cholera, tuberculosis, anthrax, and rabies. The rabies vaccine development is a fantastic story. Pasteur developed a rabies vaccine by growing the virus in rabbits. He then made the virus weak by drying the affected nerve tissue for several days. He then tested the vaccine on dogs. Tests on nine dogs were successful.

On July 6, 1885, he gave an inoculation to a nine-year-old boy, Joseph Meister, who had been badly mauled by a rabid dog. This action by Pasteur was risky, in that Pasteur was not a licensed doctor, and he could have been arrested. The lad survived, avoided contracting rabies, and lived to the age of 64. Pasteur became a national hero.

There is a sad ending to Joseph Meister, the boy Pasteur saved. Meister became a caretaker at the Pasteur Institute in Paris. He committed suicide in the gas furnace on June 24, 1940, ten days after the German Army invaded. He was consumed by guilt over having his family sent away, thinking that they had been killed. In a twist of irony fate, his family returned on the day of his suicide.

A 1936 black and white movie, "The Story of Louis Pasteur," depicts the scientist's struggles and triumphs. Turner Classic Movies (TCM) runs it periodically.

# Chapter Five

# The Science of the Heavens and Earth

## Q38: How does the Earth move?

The Earth rotates like a spinning top. The axis of spin is an imaginary line that goes through the Earth from South Pole to North Pole. It takes one day to make one spin or rotation. The axis of spin is tilted 23.5 degrees to the plane of the movement of the Earth around the Sun. That tilt gives us our seasons.

The spin or rotation means a person living near the Equator is moving 25,000 miles, which is the circumference of the Earth, in 24 hours, which figures out to about 1,000 miles per hour. People who reside about half way between the Equator and the North Pole move about 750 miles per hour.

The speed of the Earth around the Sun is 67,000 miles per hour, or about 18 miles per second. One trip around the Sun takes one year. The path, or orbit, of the Earth around the Sun is not quite a perfect circle. It is a slight oval, or ellipse, with the Earth closest to the Sun around January 4 of each year, and a bit further away on about July 5.

Our star, the Sun, is one of several hundred billion stars that make up the Milky Way Galaxy. Our Milky Way galaxy is rotating or spinning like a huge pinwheel. Our Sun, with its attendant Solar System of planets, needs about 225 million years to make one spin or one rotation.

So we're sitting on a picnic table in the park. We seem to be perfectly "still" and not moving at all. Yet we're on a spinning ball (Earth), and that ball is going around the Sun, and the Sun, plus Earth, are moving as part of a giant pinwheel. It's enough to make anybody dizzy. Yet, we do not even notice those three distinct motions. Why is that?

Gravity holds us tightly to the Earth, and we move with the Earth without noticing all that rotation and movement. Remember, those speeds are constant. We don't feel any change in speed, any acceleration or deceleration. If you are riding in a car on an extremely smooth surface, you do not feel much motion. If the car speeds up or slows down by braking, then you sure can feel the motion.

Same thing when you are flying in a regular passenger jet airplane traveling at 600 miles per hour. As long as the ride is going smoothly, it doesn't seem like you are moving. Look out the window, and you can tell you are moving over the Earth's surface. But fix your gaze inside the plane, and the sensation of motion disappears—except, of course, on take-off and landing or if you hit turbulence.

Centuries ago, people noticed the Sun, Moon, planets, and stars appeared to move around the Earth. Indeed, you and I see the Sun and Moon come up in the east and set in the west. Observers logically concluded that the Earth is stationary and the heavens move around it. This was a geocentric or earth-centered theory. It wasn't until the sixteenth century that Copernicus worked out a sun-centered or heliocentric theory, the one we subscribe to now in the 21st century.

## Q39: Why do we have different seasons?

There are three reasons for the seasons. **One**: the tilt of Earth's axis. **Two**: Earth revolves around the sun, and **Three**: the North Pole always points in the same direction. Earth's axis tilts at an angle of 23.5 degrees to the plane of revolution. When it is summer in Wisconsin, the tilt is toward the sun. Not only is the sun higher in the sky, but the sun is in the sky longer, almost 15 hours, so more heating time is allowed.

In the winter, the sun is much lower in the sky, and the sun's rays are spread out more, causing less heating. You can demonstrate this to yourself by taking a flashlight and holding it directly overhead and shining the light onto a piece of paper.

Note the size of the spot of light on the paper. Now, hold the flashlight at a very low angle and note the size of the spot of light. Yes, much more spread out. The same amount of light must now cover a larger area.

Holding the flashlight directly overhead represents summer, where the rays are more concentrated and stronger. Shining the light at a low angle is analogous to winter, where the beam is much weaker over any given area.

The Earth takes about 365 days, or one year, to go around the sun. As our Earth moves around the sun during the year, the amount of light each area of the earth receives varies. A common misconception is that the seasons are caused by the sun being closer to the Earth in the summer and farther away in the winter. And it does make sense. The closer you bring your hand to a hot plate, stove, or fire, the warmer your hand feels. But that would not account for the fact that the seasons are opposite in the Northern Hemisphere compared to the Southern Hemisphere.

The orbit of the Earth around the sun is not a perfect circle. In fact, the path is slightly oval or elliptical. The sun is closest (perihelion) to the Earth about January 4th of each year and the farthest away (aphelion) on about July 5. The difference is only about 3 million miles out of a total of 93 million miles, and that difference would not account for the change in seasons.

In the Northern Hemisphere during summer, the North Pole points toward the sun. The highest the sun gets above the southern horizon in the mid latitudes at noon is close to 72 degrees on June 21, the summer solstice. The Sun is so high it seems to be almost overhead. On the day of the winter solstice, December 21, in the Northern Hemisphere the sun is only about 25 degrees above the southern horizon at noon. That low sun angle does not allow much heating for the Earth. In short, the seasons are not caused by the closeness of earth to the sun, but rather by the 23.5 degree tilt of Earth on its axis.

There is another factor to consider. The Northern Hemisphere is dominated by large land masses, while the Southern Hemisphere has large ocean areas. Those large land areas in our hemisphere tend to make winters colder and summers hotter. Why is that? Land heats up more easily than water. So the large land masses of North America heat up more in our summer, compared to the summers in the Southern Hemisphere.

We see this effect on a smaller scale by observing deserts in California. The daytime temperatures in the Mojave Desert can get well above 100 degrees, but at night the temperature dips to near freezing. By contrast, night and day temperatures along the California coast do not vary nearly as much.

## Q40: Why is Earth the only planet to support life?

While there may be life on distant planets around faraway stars, Earth is the only life-supporting planet we know of yet. And why is that? Five good reasons! First, Earth has liquid water, the most essential ingredient for life. Earth is the perfect distance from the Sun for water to exist in all three states, solid ice, liquid water, and vapor or gas. Water contains oxygen needed for life, it doesn't harm the skin, and it's needed for photosynthesis. Photosynthesis is the process of turning water and carbon dioxide, with the aid of light, into oxygen and sugars used as plant food. Water is drinkable, and permits molecules to move around easily. Mercury and Venus are so close to the Sun that liquid water would boil away. The planet Mars, and Titan, a moon of Saturn, may have water below the surface, but that's only speculation.

Second, our atmosphere is ideal. It contains breathable oxygen, left there as the byproduct of plant growth. Our atmosphere has some carbon dioxide, which animals and humans give off as part of respiration. The tiny bit of carbon dioxide helps moderate the temperature of Earth. Mars, Mercury, and the Moon are too small to keep an atmosphere. You need enough gravity, and Earth has it. As a bonus, Earth's atmosphere is thick enough to filter out many harmful ultraviolet rays. Our magnetic field deflects tons of particles from the Sun that would otherwise kill us in short order.

Third, Earth is blessed with a beautiful climate. The temperature is ideal for life. Mercury and Venus are too close to the Sun, and go from 600 degrees above zero Fahrenheit to 400 degrees below zero Fahrenheit. Those extremes are not conducive to life. Mars is a tad less extreme, but at 140 degrees below zero Fahrenheit at times, water and blood would freeze. The outer planets have no solid surface and are way too cold.

Fourth, Earth receives sufficient light for trees and other plants to produce oxygen by the process of photosynthesis. The Earth's rotation, once every 24 hours, insures that each side of the planet receives sunlight on a regular basis. Venus takes 243 days to spin once on its axis. Any place on Venus is in darkness far too long to support vegetation and life.

Fifth, the earth's magnetic field protects us from dangerous radiation. That magnetic field deflects the solar particles streaming from the sun. We witness the protection of the earth's magnetic field when solar particles strike oxygen and nitrogen in the upper atmosphere and give us the Northern Lights or aurora borealis.

Recall the Goldilocks and Three Bears bedtime story. The porridge was too hot, too cold, and just right. The armchairs were too hard, too soft, and just right. The bed was too high, too low, and just right. Goldilocks wisely chose the "just right' version each time.

Earth is "just right" in terms of location, size, rotation rate, mass, gravity, water, atmosphere, climate, and magnetic field.

So far, we've been discussing life in our solar system, which is a tiny little corner of the Universe. Is there life on other planets in distant solar systems? Most scientists think the answer is yes, but there is no proof. For now, our Earth is all we know, and we had best take good care of it.

## Q41: How much longer will Earth exist?

Most scientists expect Earth to survive about another five billion years. The earth has already been around for almost five billion years, so it's middle-aged. Most scientists believe that our sun and planets were formed at the same time from a huge cloud of dust and gas. The cloud shrank under the pull of its own gravity, forming the sun and a disk of material that swirled around the sun. Friction caused the disk to collect into huge whirlpools that formed into planets.

The earth is a vibrant and dynamic planet. It is always changing, with the surface crust moving around on huge plates. Continents connect and separate. Climate and weather sculpt Earth's features. But the ultimate fate of the earth is determined by the sun.

The sun is an ordinary star in a Milky Way galaxy that is made up of 100 billion stars. Stars are born, live out their lifetimes, and die. The fate of any star depends on its mass. Massive stars end up as supernovas that may create black holes. Small stars end up as big pieces of cinder. Our sun is a medium size star.

Like all stars, our sun converts hydrogen to helium. This fusion will continue until the hydrogen fuel is all gone. The sun in now in a stable state, where gravity wants to make it smaller and radiation wants to push it outward. These two forces are now in balance.

But look out! Danger is just around the corner! In about five billion years, the core will contract and get hotter, causing the sun's outer layers to expand. The sun will expand to the red giant stage and engulf the inner planets of Mercury, Venus, Earth, and Mars. Earth will have a fiery death, and all earthly life will cease.

If you look in the constellation of Orion, you can see the reddish star Betelgeuse that is right above the belt of Orion. Betelgeuse is a sun like ours that is now in the red giant stage. Below the belt of Orion is a hot young blue-white star named Rigel. Rigel is a baby in the evolution of stars.

## Q42: *How far is it to the horizon?*

A few weeks ago, I ran into a friend who told me about fishing nine miles off shore where the water was 450 feet deep. He said he could see the shoreline from his boat and wondered if there was a way to determine the distance to the horizon, the line where the sky meets the water.

From the diagram below, let h equal the height of a person, R the radius of the Earth and d the distance to the horizon. From the Pythagorean Theorem, we can come up with a rule that says $d^2 = 2Rh$, or in language terms: d equals the square root of the product of 2, R, and h.

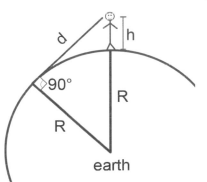

Let's say my friend is standing at the water's edge (shoreline) and his eyes are 6 feet above the water level of the lake or ocean. So h is 6

ft. (6 feet = .0011 miles) The radius of the Earth is 4000 miles. The horizon distance, d, works out to be 3 miles. So, if you're standing at the shoreline, you can see 3 miles out to sea.

Let's try another example. You're at the top of the 1600 foot Willis Tower (formerly Sears Tower) in Chicago. How far out onto Lake Michigan can you see? So h is 1600 feet (or .3 miles), R is 4000 miles, and d works out to about 50 miles.

There is another derived formula that can be used: d equals 1.22 times the square root of h. Again d is the distance in miles to the horizon, and h is the distance in feet that the person's eyes are above the water or shoreline.

Can you see any further by using binoculars or a telescope? The answer is no. The horizon may be a little sharper, but it isn't any greater distance away. My friend's ability to see farther is limited by the earth's curvature.

Although my friend could only see three miles to the horizon where water met the sky, he did see the shoreline 9 miles away. Why? It's because hills and trees stick quite far up above the line where the water meets the land. In fact, if the treetops on shore are hundred feet above the lake level, you should be able to see them from twelve miles out to sea.

As a matter of historical interest, one of the first proofs that the Earth might be round was the fact that the last visible part of any sailing ship leaving port was the top of the sailing mast.

## Q43: *What causes fog?*

Fog is actually a cloud at ground level. Fog is made up of condensed water droplets. It is caused by air being cooled to the point where it can no longer hold water in the invisible vapor form. Cool air cannot hold the moisture that warm air can.

The water vapor condenses onto particles of dust, ice, salt, and oxygen molecules, or actually most anything that is in the air. The word condense means to change from a vapor or gas state to a liquid state of matter. It is those tiny water droplets that we call fog.

Several mechanisms can give us fog. **One**: A cool, stable air mass is trapped below a warmer air mass. **Two**: Rain cools and moistens the air near the ground until fog forms. **Three**: On a cloud-free night, a humid air mass cools due to infrared radiation. This occurs most often in the fall, when land and water have warmed up during the summer and are still evaporating tons of water into the air. **Four**: A warm, moist air mass blows across a cold surface, such as snow, ice, or ocean. This is called advection fog and can often be found along the western coast of the United States.

Fog usually forms when the temperature of the air and the dew point temperature are within about three to four degrees Fahrenheit. The dew point is the temperature at which the air can no longer hold moisture.

On a typical summer day, the air cools as night comes on. When the temperature drops sufficiently to reach the dew point temperature, the cool air can no longer be held in a vapor state, and it condenses on the grass in what we call dew.

Fog is a really fast way to melt snow. We saw this in our Tomah area in the third week in February. A humid, warm air mass drawn up from the South rode over the snow. The colder snow cooled this warm air. Recall that cooler air can't hold the moisture that warm air can. Fog forms at the surface of the snow. Condensation itself is a warming process and that helps melt the snow.

The foggiest place in the United States is off Point Reyes, California. It gets over 200 foggy days every year. This weather occurs due to advection fog when warm air moves over upwelling cooler Pacific Ocean water.

Valley fog is caused by colder heavy air settling into valleys, while warmer air forms above it. We often see this in our southwestern part of Wisconsin along the Kickapoo, Wisconsin, and Mississippi Rivers. Sunlight will usually burn off the fog by mid-morning.

Artificial fog for theatre and movie work is made by heating a water and glycerin (glycol) fluid mixture. The vapors are forced out of an exit and upon contact with cooler room air quickly condense on particles in the air, producing a fog.

## Q44: How does lightning form?

Lightning is an electrical discharge between oppositely charged objects. Those two oppositely charged objects may be clouds, as in cloud-to-cloud lightning. Or they may be a cloud and the ground, as in cloud-to-ground lightning. Clouds are made of particles. Friction occurs when those particles slide over each other. Friction causes objects to become charged. One object becomes negatively charged and the other is positively charge. We experience tiny lightning discharges when we remove a sweater in dry winter air or slide our feet across the carpet and touch a doorknob.

Lightning from over 1800 thunderstorms strikes the Earth a hundred times every second. Lightning may have played a role in creating early life forms by breaking down amino acids into gases such as ammonia, hydrogen, methane and water vapor. Lightning may have also insured humans' early survival by providing them with fire. Lightning establishes the negative electric charge needed to produce nitrogen that plants need.

A stroke of lightning can produce as much as 100 million volts and 20 million amps. The air around a lightning stroke is heated so rapidly it expands faster than sound travels, which leads to a sonic boom or what we call thunder.

There has been a long-standing controversy on whether lightning went from cloud to ground or from ground to cloud. Research has shown that there is normally a small, nearly invisible leader stroke from cloud to ground, followed by the brilliant return stroke from ground to cloud.

You can tell how far lightning is away from you by using the five-second rule. Count the time between lightning flash and the sound of the thunder. Divide that number of seconds by five to get the distance in miles. Sound travels about 1100 feet in one second or about one mile in five seconds. Let's say, for example, you count ten seconds between flash and thunder. If you divide ten by five, you find the lightning is two miles from you.

## Q45: *Why are there so many tornados in Texas and Oklahoma?*
. . . . . . . . . . . . . . . . . . . . . . . . . . . . . . . . . . . . . . . .

Texas and Oklahoma are big states with lots of area to generate a ton of tornadoes. As a matter of fact, the urban area of Oklahoma City has been hit over 100 times by tornadoes

About 1,000 tornadoes strike the United States every year, killing an average of 60 people. No other country has as many violent twisters as we have here in the United States.

We owe this distinction to the unique geography of our great country. Tornadoes move out in front of a line of thunderstorms, called a squall line. These Great Plain thunderstorms are caused by warm moist air being pulled up off the waters of the Gulf of

Mexico, plus hot dry air coming up north off the land mass of Texas and Mexico. Cold air comes down from Canada. When these air masses meet, the result is trouble and violence.

The warm air at lower altitudes starts rising. Cool air at the higher altitudes descends. As these two air masses try to pass each other, the Earth's rotation tends to start the air masses twisting or turning in a counterclockwise direct in our Northern Hemisphere. The result is a twisting, twirling "rope" of air moving from the southwest to the northeast with a speed that varies from zero mph to 40 mph. The most destructive tornadoes are created from super cells or rotating thunderstorms. The F scale, developed by Dr. T. Theodore Fujita at the University of Chicago, relates the degree of damage due to wind speed. The really, really bad tornadoes are ones that get an F-5 rating.

There are some tornado myths. One such myth is that tornados are attracted to mobile homes. Not true. It's just that mobile homes are more vulnerable to damaging winds. Another myth is that tornados do not hit at places where three rivers meet. Yes, they do, and there is documentation to prove it.

The most devastating tornado in history was the F-5 Tri-state tornado that occurred on March 25, 1925. Winds speeds were from 261 to 318 miles per hour. The tornado killed about 700 people along a 219-mile track across Missouri, Illinois, and Indiana. Another storm, the infamous Easter Sunday, 1974 two-day outbreak of 147 tornadoes killed 310 people throughout the Midwest.

The tornado "season" starts in January and February in Florida. Tornado frequency peaks in the southern states, along the Gulf Coast, in May and June. In the upper Midwest, peak season is June, July and August.

Tornado Alley refers to that broad swath of high tornado occurrences in the central United State, right up through Oklahoma, Kansas, and Nebraska.

## Q46: Why is the sky blue?

. . . . . . . . . . . . . . . . . . . . . . .

If the sky was green, you wouldn't know when to stop mowing!! Just a little joke. Actually this is an excellent question.

Light travels in a straight line unless it hits something. Light can do three things when it strikes an object. It can reflect like a mirror. It can refract or bend as it would in a prism. It can scatter by hitting tiny particles and molecules in the air.

Light is really made up of seven colors. An easy way to remember them is: ROY G BIV for red, orange, yellow, green, blue, indigo, violet. Frankly, we don't see indigo, and it's tough to see the orange. Isaac Newton identified five colors, and later added the orange and indigo. His reasoning was that seven colors was an analogy to the seven notes on the musical scale, the seven known planets at the time, the seven days of the week.

The shortest light waves are blue and the longest are red. When light travels through our atmosphere, some of the light is scattered. Dust particles and moisture act as tiny mirrors and reflect light in all directions. The shorter blue waves are scattered the most which means we see these reflections from dust particles and moisture. The short blue waves are scattered about ten times more than the longer red rays. So we say the sky looks blue.

When we look at the sky close to the horizon, we see the sky is a lighter blue or even a white color. The light hitting our eye from so low on the horizon has passed through a lot more atmosphere than light overhead. The dust particles and air molecules have scattered and re-scattered the blue light many, many times in many directions. The surface of the Earth has reflected much light. All that scattering combines the colors again and we tend to see all the waves which yield white or light blue.

Try this easy science experiment. Fill a large glass bowl or small fish aquarium with water. Add a few drops of milk to the water. It might help to use a medicine dropper. Shine a strong flashlight through the bowl or aquarium from the side. Notice the color of the water. It looks mostly blue. If you look at the water in line with the flashlight, the water looks reddish. All the blue has been scattered out and only red is left. That is the reason that sunrises and sunsets are a reddish color.

## Q47: Why are raindrops round?

Ah, an excellent question, so simple and graceful. During his Miracle Year (Annus Mirabilis) of 1905, Albert Einstein wrote four major papers: The Photoelectric Effect, Brownian Motion, Special Relativity, and Mass-Energy Equivalence. His 1921 Nobel Prize was for his explanation of the photoelectric effect.

Decades later, Einstein was asked why he, rather than other scientists, was successful in uncovering the secrets of the universe. He gave two reasons. First, "I never gave up, I was as stubborn as a mule," and secondly, "I always asked the simplest questions, the kind that children ask. I ask them still." It is these "children's questions" that underlie some of the most deep and profound mysteries of the world around us.

In the case of raindrops, the secret is surface tension, which is the cohesion of water. Molecules that are alike tend to stick together. The cause is the weak hydrogen bonds that occur between water molecules. The surface tension of water acts as a thin film-like membrane. This allows a person to place a needle or paper clip on water and not have it fall through, even though steel is eight times denser than water. Surface tension also allows those water strider or skeeter bugs to stay atop the water surface.

Surface tension always works to make the smallest surface area possible. There's some neat math here. A sphere is the geometric figure that has the least surface area for any given volume. Surface tension, like cohesion, will pull any liquid into a round or spherical shape.

Raindrops start out high in the sky as water vapor condenses and collects on dust, smoke, or oxygen molecules. Tiny falling raindrops are round. But raindrops collide on the way down, and become bigger. Falling through the air and encountering air resistance, raindrops lose their round shape. They become more like the top half of a hamburger bun, flattened on the bottom, with a curved dome top. That teardrop shape, popular with artists, weather forecast maps, and television weather reports, is clearly wrong.

The Earth and other planets have a spherical shape for the same reason that raindrops are round. The Earth and the other solid planets were liquid when they formed. Surface tension and gravity force fluids, including planets and stars, into spheres. Stars, like the Sun, are round for the same reason. A sphere, or ball, is the figure that has the least surface area.

Some of the smaller moons of Jupiter and Saturn, and the rocks that make up the rings of planets, plus asteroids, are not spherical. They are misshapen and deformed chunks of material. They were never liquid when they formed.

The beauty and elegance of science is using the same physical principles to explain a variety of phenomena that are seemingly unrelated.

Larry Scheckel

## Q48: Why doesn't the longest day of the year have the earliest sunrise?

• • • • • • • • • • • • • • • • • • • • • • • • • • • • • • • • • • • • • • • • • • • • • • •

The common wisdom is that June 21, the summer solstice, is the longest day of the year and that December 21, the winter solstice, is the shortest day of the year. And that is true.

To get the shortest possible day (daylight), we want a late sunrise and early sunset. The dates of latest sunrise and earliest sunset depend on latitude. Here's what happens in Tomah, Wisconsin. The latest sunrise is January 3 at 7:37 AM. The earlier sunset is December 9 at about 4:24 PM.

Up to December 9, the sunrise gets later and sunsets earlier, so the days shorten. From December 9 to December 21, sunsets get later, and sunrises also get later, but sunrise advances faster than sunset, so days continue to get shorter.

From December 21, the solstice, to January 3, both sunrise and sunset continue to get later, but sunset advances faster, so the days get longer. After January 3, sunrise switches direction and begins to come earlier, while sunset grows later, so each day is longer. December 21 (sometimes December 22) remains the shortest day of the year, with about 9 hours of daylight and 15 hours of darkness.

Why aren't the latest sunrise and earliest sunset on the same day, namely December 21, the winter solstice?

Two factors are involved. First, the Earth's axis is tilted 23.5 degrees with respect to its plane of orbit around the sun. Second, the Earth's orbit around the sun is not a perfect circle, but rather an ellipse or oval shape. It is the first factor—the tilt—that is most important.

The time of day when the sun gets to its highest point in the sky is called solar noon, and the time from one solar noon to the next one is called the solar day. The length of the solar day is not constant throughout the year. Around the winter and summer solstices (Dec 21 and June 21), it is a tad more than 24 hours, and near the spring and fall equinoxes (Mar 21 and Sept 21), it is slightly less than 24 hours.

The length of the solar day is determined mostly by the rotation of the Earth on its axis, and a little bit by its revolution around the sun.

We don't like to tell time using solar days, because we want every day to be the same, exactly 24 hours. So our clocks don't run on solar time. Our clocks average out the variations in the solar day, making every day the same length, so our clocks don't entirely agree with the solar day.

Solar noon rarely occurs exactly at clock noon. During the winter solstice, solar noon occurs at a slightly later time each day because the solar day is slightly more than 24 hours. So when we talk about "earliest sunset," we mean earliest according to our constantly running clocks. The difference between clock time and solar time creates the phenomenon. If sundials were used to tell time, the latest sunrise and earliest sunset would occur on December 21, the winter solstice.

### Q49: How do rainbows form, and why do we see them only after rainstorms?

Rainbows are formed by sunlight and water droplets from rain. The great seventeenth century scientist Isaac Newton was the first to prove that sunlight is made up of seven colors: red, orange, green, blue, indigo, and violet. Well, actually six, as it's difficult to see any indigo. Newton let sunlight pass through a triangular piece of glass called a prism and split into different colors.

Raindrops both reflect and refract (bend) sunlight. As a ray of sunlight enters a raindrop, it is refracted or bent. Since violet is a shorter wave than red, it bends the most. Most of the sunlight passes right through the raindrop, but a small amount reflects off the inside back of the drop, and then bends again as exits the drop. Millions of these raindrops, refracting and separating light into a spectrum, give us the rainbow.

Rainbows are usually seen in the east in the late afternoon after a thunderstorm has moved through. The sunlight must be to your back. You can create your own rainbow with a garden hose, and you can often see a rainbow around waterfalls.

Do try this science experiment. Make your own rainbow. Fill a dish with water and rest a flat mirror against one side of the dish. Orient the dish so that sunlight comes through a window and falls on the mirror. Hold a white sheet of paper vertically and several feet away from the dish. Adjust the dish, mirror, and white sheet of paper so that a rainbow of colors falls on the white sheet. The wedge of water acts as a prism and splits the light into the seven colors. Red is bent or refracted the least and violet is bent the most.

## Q50: How do clouds form, and how do clouds get their color?

Clouds are bunches of very tiny water droplets. The droplets are so light and small that they can float in the air. Clouds form when warm air rises, expands, and cools. The warm air has some moisture in it, but it is in vapor form and cannot be seen. The rising air cools about 3.5 degrees Fahrenheit for every thousand feet in altitude, a pace referred to as the adiabatic cooling rate. The lifted air is cooled to its dew point temperature, the temperature at which air is completely saturated. The air can no longer retain its vapor. The relative humidity has reached 100 percent.

Cool air cannot hold as much vapor as warm air. The vapor condenses onto dust particles and oxygen molecules. Most of these particles come from cars, trucks, volcanoes, and forest fires. Condense means to change from a gas state to a liquid state. Billions and billions of these tiny droplets come together and form what we see as a visible cloud. At the highest altitudes, the tiny droplets will freeze and form ice crystals.

So why are clouds white? Clouds are white because they reflect light from the sun. Light from the sun is made of the seven colors of red, orange, yellow, green, blue, indigo, and violet (ROYBIV). Clouds reflect those seven colors evenly, in about the same amount, to give white light. It's actually six colors, because Isaac Newton put indigo in that mixture. Indigo is not easy to see and is no longer considered one of the colors of the rainbow.

We see grayish or dark-looking clouds when the cloud cover is very thick, because not as much sunlight is getting through the clouds. Thunderstorm clouds build up so high in the atmosphere that the clouds take on a blackish appearance.

Cloud height is determined by the type of cloud and the size of the tiny water droplets that make up the cloud. Those fluffy white cumulus clouds with the flat bottoms generally have the heftiest water droplets, so those clouds are found at about 3,000 to 12,000 feet above the ground. Clouds move along with the wind. Cumulus clouds move about 10 to 20 miles per hour, but faster with thunderstorms.

Those very high thin wispy clouds or cirrus clouds, often called mare's tails, are composed of very small ice crystals and are spotted at about 30,000 feet above the ground. Those high cirrus clouds are pushed by the jet stream and clock in at over 100 miles per hour. Cirrus clouds indicate that a change in weather is fast approaching.

Fog is a special kind of cloud. Most fog forms when warm moisture-laden air flows over a colder surface. If the air is full of moisture, it will condense onto particles in the air.

Besides cumulus and cirrus clouds, there are stratus clouds. Stratus refers to layers, so these stratus clouds stretch out over great distances in the sky. Stratus clouds yield a long steady rain, rather than a cloudburst that can occur from cumulonimbus clouds.

As a general rule, we tend to see many cumulus clouds in summer and a preponderance of stratus clouds in winter.

# Chapter Six

# Art, Music, Sports and Math

found an advantage to a bit of color.

Doctors stare at red blood for a long time under bright lights. Seeing blue-green scrubs refreshes a doctor's vision of red things, like the bloody organs she encounters during surgery. Staring at that red under very bright lights desensitizes vision to red color. If the doctor looked up and saw an assistant's white scrub suit, there would be a disturbing blue-green (called cyan) afterimage. But if the assistant's clothes are already blue-green, the afterimage is barely noticeable.

You might try this. Cut out a heart from a glossy bright green paper and a yellow border and mount them on a light gray paper. Put a small black dot in the center. Make a dot in the center of a sheet of plain white paper. Stare at the heart for thirty seconds, focusing on the black dot. Do not blink.

After thirty seconds, transfer your gaze to the dot on the plain white paper and focus on the black dot. After staring at the green and yellow heart, you should see an afterimage of a red heart.

## Q53: Why do bottles make a noise when you blow over them?

Bottles, like pop bottles, catsup bottles, and wine bottles, make that noise for the same reason that church pipe organs work: resonance. The bottle becomes a pipe whose length is determined by how much soda or water is in the bottle. There is an equation that determines the note or pitch you hear. Basically, the wavelength of the sound is four times the length of the closed pipe (pop bottle).

There is another equation that relates the main three properties of any wave. The three properties are wavelength, wave velocity or speed, and the frequency. Frequency and pitch mean the same, which is the number of vibrations per second.

Another equation relates wavelength to frequency. The equation states that the wavelength is equal to the velocity divided by the frequency.

A foot-long pop bottle will produce a pitch or note of about 250 Hz or C on the piano keyboard. The longer the bottle or organ pipe, the lower the note, pitch, or frequency of the sound.

There are basically three ways to get sound from a pop bottle. One way is to blow across the top, as mentioned above. Another is to rap the bottle. Hold the blade of a heavy table knife and rap the handle against the bottle. The pitch or note you get depends on how much water is in the bottle. But the results are opposite to blowing across the top. In other words, the more water the pop bottle contains, the lower the pitch. That's because there is more mass, and something with more mass will vibrate at a lower pitch.

New York City's St. Luke's Bottle Band is on television every year around Christmas. They are a real treat to watch and hear. Some members of the Bottle Band blow across the top, some rap with a metal mallet, and some hook a finger in the opening and sort of 'pluck' it. With different size bottles and varying amounts of water, most all pitches or frequencies are produced. They are a big hit and have a wonderful sound!

Try this experiment with sound. Take two identical glass bottles, such as pop bottles, and fill them with different amounts of water. Use the handle end of a knife to rap the side of each bottle. Which one has the higher note or pitch?

Now, blow over the top of each bottle. Which bottle now has the higher pitch? When you rap the side of the bottle, you get a low pitch because the larger amount of water vibrates more slowly. When you blow across the top, the air inside the bottle vibrates. The bottle with the most water makes for a shorter vibrating air column and hence a higher pitch. It is the same principle used in church pipe organs.

## Q54: Why does a siren get higher-pitched as it approaches and lower-pitched as it gets further away?

This phenomenon is known as the Doppler Effect, after Christian Doppler, an Austrian physicist who discovered it in 1842. Sound waves travel through the air like water waves roll through the ocean. The closer together the waves are, the higher the pitch or frequency. The farther apart the waves are, the lower the pitch. As the siren approaches you, the waves are compressed, so you hear a higher pitch. As the siren passes, the waves are spread out behind it and you hear a lower-pitched sound. Another way to think about it is that when the siren approaches you, you intercept more waves each second and hear a higher pitch. When the siren moves away from you, fewer waves reach you each second, so you hear a lower pitch.

The Doppler Effect is the basis of police radar. The police car antenna transmits radio waves. The waves bounce off the speeding vehicle and return to the antenna. The radar unit compares the difference between the sent and received waves and translates that information into miles per hour.

By the way, I think it is easier to experience the Doppler Effect by listening to a motorcycle going by. Try closing your eyes to eliminate visual cues and just listening to the Doppler Effect.

## Q55: What are guitar strings made of?

Early guitars, going back to the year 1265 AD, used strings made from catgut. Despite their name, catgut strings are actually made from sheep intestines. The same "catgut" is used for medical sutures in surgery and strings for tennis rackets. Nylon guitar strings were introduced in 1946.

Steel guitar strings came out when Fender and Gibson produced electric guitars. The first two strings (the bottom two, which are for high pitches) are made of plain steel. They look like steel, sort of a gray color. The other four strings are made from Bronze Wound. They have, as the name implies, a steel core with bronze wire wrapped around. A Bronze Wound string appears amber in color. The thinner steel core string is under tension and the Bronze Wound increases the mass of the string. These strings vary in size (gauge) depending on the note the string is asked to produce.

Some guitarists use "phosphor bronze" instead of plain bronze strings. These strings offer a brighter note, and slightly different tonal flavor or quality. Other classical guitars use six steel strings. They are easier to play.

An acoustic guitar is a hollow-bodied guitar that does not have electric amplification. The top plate of a quality acoustic guitar is made of spruce or cedar. The backs and sides are made of Brazilian rosewood. Rosewood is very dense and hard and tends to contribute to a sweeter note. Rosewood can't be imported into the United States anymore, so woods from Mexico and Hawaii are now being used.

The sound from a guitar is produced by the vibration of the strings which is amplified by the wooden body of the guitar.

Electric guitars produce sound by string vibration in the same manner as acoustic guitars. However, a piezo-electric or magnetic pickup transforms the movement of the string to an electrical signal, which is then amplified.

Metal inserts, called frets, are inset in a fret board on the neck of the guitar. The raised edges of the frets provide fixed lengths

120 pounds on Earth would weigh about 20 pounds on the Moon.

Physicists have calculated that a golf ball hit on the Moon should be in the air for 70 seconds and go 2.5 miles. There is no air on the Moon, so there is no air resistance. The ball would not be slowed down by running into air molecules. The best angle to hit the ball would be 45 degrees. The ball coming off the Moon tee would be traveling 180 miles per hour.

Some assumptions must be made. In a bulky astronaut suit, it is very difficult to get the kind of dynamic swing one could make here on Earth.

Also, the dimples on a golf ball are useless on the Moon. Those dimples grab some of the air clinging next to the ball and mix it with the fast-moving air going around the ball. Dimples give the ball extra lift. There is no such lift on the Moon, as there is no air.

In February, 1971, Alan Shepard became the fifth man to walk on the Moon. He took two golf balls and the head of a Wilson 6 iron golf club with him. While on the Moon, Shepard taped the golf head to a lunar sample tool and hit the two golf balls, swinging the club with only one arm. The second one he jokingly said went "miles and miles and miles." In fact, it went a few hundred feet at best. The astronaut space suit was so confining, Shepard could only produce a very weak swing.

What about terminal velocity? An object dropped from a height of several miles here on Earth will go faster and faster until the force of air resistance upward is equal to the force of gravity downward. When those two forces are equal, the ball does not go any faster. We say it no longer accelerates. It falls at a constant speed, which is termed "terminal velocity."

A human, jumping out of an airplane without pulling the parachute, will have a terminal velocity of about 120 miles per hour. It would take him about ten seconds to speed up and fall a distance of about 1,000 ft. A golf ball, dropped from a great height above the earth will have a terminal velocity of around 200 miles per hour.

An object dropped on the Moon will not have any terminal velocity. Because there is no air on the Moon, the ball will go faster and faster (accelerate) until it strikes the surface of the Moon.

You might want to try this cool science exercise. Stand on a chair or stepladder and drop one of those flared coffee filters. Notice that it reaches its terminal velocity, or maximum speed, quickly and within a few inches of release. For the rest of the distance, it falls at the same rate. The weight downward (force of gravity) is equal to the force of air resistance upward. No further acceleration takes place.

## Q58: *What is the greatest distance a home run can possibly be hit?*

New York Yankee great Mickey Mantle hit a 565-foot home run at Griffith Stadium in Washington, DC on April 17, 1953. That home run remains baseball's official record holder.

Is that the longest home run possible? Or perhaps the question should be posed as: What is a practical limit to home run distance? There are many variables.

Foremost, a batter wants the ball pitched at the highest possible speed. The ball's forward energy will be returned when it bounces off the bat. Consider this idea. The harder you throw a ball at a wall, the faster it will come back to you. The batter wants a really fast pitch.

What is the fastest pitch possible? A number of pitchers in the major leagues are throwing at 100-plus miles per hour. A select few, Verlander, Herrera, Mayberry, and Parnell, have been clocked in the 101 to 102 mph range. The record is held by Aroldis Chapman of the Cincinnati Reds at 105 mph.

Anything over 110 mph is going to result in a torn rotator cuff, dislocated shoulder, or pulling a tendon from bone. The limiting factor is not muscle, or conditioning, or technique. It's pure anatomy. So let's use a 110-mph fastball pitch.

The second major factor to insure a long home run is bat speed. The hitter wants the bat moving at the highest possible speed, with the ball hitting the sweet spot of the bat. Timers clocked the bat speed of Albert Pujols, Cardinal great, now with the Los Angeles Angels, at nearly 120 mph. A bat speed of 125 mph is not unreasonable.

The ideal hitter would weigh about 245 pounds and stand 6 feet, 7 inches tall. He would have long arms, a swift forward stride, excellent upper body strength, and a quick wrist snap.

So far, we have a fireball pitcher throwing 110 mph and a powerful hitter swinging the lumber at 125 mph. We want a launch angle of about 35 degrees. Some backspin on the ball will give the baseball additional lift.

Air resistance or air friction will slow the batted ball down. Dry air will cause less friction than humid air. Cold air is denser than warm air. We're asking for warm air, about 75 degrees Fahrenheit. We prefer thin air, so a high-altitude ball park is best. Coors Field, home of the Colorado Rockies, would suffice. We'll assume no wind. Once again, the ideal ballpark conditions are warm and dry air, at a high-altitude ballpark.

In his book, *The Physics of Baseball*, author Robert Adair puts all those conditions into mathematical equations and calculates that the ball will leave the bat at a speed of 194 mph, stay in the air for 9.3 seconds, and land 748 feet from home plate.

Given all the above ideal conditions, the longest home run it is possible to hit is 748 feet. Do not hold your breath. Home runs of 500 feet are rare today, even as athletes are bigger, stronger, and in better physical condition than in decades past.

## Q59: What are Fibonacci numbers?
· · · · · · · · · · · · · · · · · · · · · · · · · · · · ·

A Fibonacci sequence goes like this: 1, 1, 2, 3, 5, 8, 13, 21, 34, 55, 89. Each successive number is the sum of the two preceding numbers. So 1+1 =2 and 1+2=3 and 2+3=5. Leonardo Fibonacci was born in 1175 in Pisa, Italy and is responsible for changing the number system from Roman numerals to our current Hindu-Arabic system.

The scales or bracts of pinecones, sunflower seeds in the sunflower head, pineapple scales, flower petals, and finger lengths between joints are all examples of Fibonacci sequences.

Fibonacci numbers are involved in rabbit reproduction, and can also be tied to the reproduction of cows and bees. Here is an example: If a cow produces its first she calf at age two years and after that produces another single she-calf every year, how many she-calves are there after twelve years, assuming none die?

The answer is 233. If you start with just the one cow and start time at year 0, then in years 0 and 1 there is only that one cow. Those are the first two numbers in the sequence: 1 and 1. Then in year 2 that cow has a calf, and the population is now 2, which is the third number in the sequence. In year 3, the original cow has another calf, plus the calf from year 2, giving a total population of 3, the fourth number in the sequence. In year 4, the original cow has another calf, plus the calf born in year 2 now bears a calf of her own, and there's still that calf from year 3, bringing the total population to 5. If you continue the pattern, it's just a matter of finding the 13th Fibonacci number because we started with year 0, so the 13th number would be the population after year 12. The numbers add up to 233.

The Greeks' Golden Ratio of 1.618 comes from dividing any two successive Fibonacci numbers. For example, 89 divided by 55 is 1.618. Greek statues and artwork used this special ratio.

You might want to try this. Measure the lengths between the joints of your finger. The smallest length added to the next longest length adds up to the third and longest length. For example: 1 inch + 1.5 inches = 2.5 inches.

### Q60: What mistakes can happen if you don't make the proper metric conversion?

In July, 1983 a brand-new Boeing 767, the most advanced jetliner in the world, crash-landed in Canada. It ran out of fuel on a flight from Montreal to Edmonton. Ground crews who refueled the plane had found the fuel gauge did not work. So the crew manually checked with a drip stick, which is similar to the dip stick we use to check the oil level in our car. The dip procedure displayed fuel in liters. Air Canada had changed from recording fuel in pounds to fuel in kilograms.

The First Officer, Maurice Quintal, told the refueling crew the conversion factor was 1.77. But what units go with 1.77? The ground crew used the value of 1.77 without being certain of the units. The density of jet fuel happens to be 1.77 pounds per liter. The end result was that they added 5000 liters when they should have added 20,000 liters. Flight 143, with 61 passengers on board, ran out of fuel at 26,000 feet and glided powerless for 29 minutes to an emergency landing at Winnipeg. The captain, a former glider pilot in WWII, crashed landed on an abandoned Air Force base runway. Everyone got out safely.

The crew got all mixed up in the conversion between liters, kilograms, and pounds. In physics and chemistry classes, we spend considerable time converting and making sure the units cancel. The metric system requires very little math manipulation, because it is based on multiplying by 10. Another reason why we in the United States should go metric!

NASA lost a $125 million dollar spacecraft, the Mars Climate Orbiter. One team from NASA's Jet Propulsion Lab in Pasadena was using the metric system (meters, kilograms, Celsius) and another team was applying the English system (feet, miles, pounds, Fahrenheit).

The spacecraft was supposed to fire its braking rocket on September 23, 1999 to put it into orbit 90 miles above the surface of Mars. Instead, the craft went into a 35-mile high orbit, which was too low, and it burned up. Once again we see the folly of having two different systems of measurement.

Based on multiplying by factors of 10, the metric system is simpler, easy to use, and more logical. Our military uses the metric system, as do commercial airlines, the liquor industry, and most of the industrialized world. International sporting events, like the Olympic Games, are conducted using metric measurements.

Canada "went metric" in 1970. We in the United States put ourselves at a disadvantage by hanging on to the antiquated and cumbersome English system. Mechanics have to buy two sets of socket wrenches and other tools. United States businesses and manufacturers lose trade because of our cumbersome English system. Occasionally we lose an expensive spacecraft, and we risk losing lives.

# Chapter Seven

# Incredible Technology

## Q61: *How does electricity work?*
. . . . . . . . . . . . . . . . . . . . . . . . . . .

Everything is made of atoms. Atoms have a dense positive center called the nucleus. Zooming around the nucleus are smaller and less dense particles called electrons. These electrons orbit the nucleus much as planets orbit the sun.

We get electricity when we make the electrons move away from the nucleus and start traveling or migrating in a conductor, such as a piece of wire. The movement of the electrons is called current. The force that gets those electrons moving is called voltage.

Ben Franklin was the first to give the names positive and negative to electricity. If there are too many electrons, we have a negative charge. If there are not enough electrons, we have a positive charge.

There are several ways to get those electrons moving. If a conductor (wire) is moved through a magnetic field, electrons will start moving in the wire. That is how we get most of the electricity we use in our homes, businesses, and factories. This process is called electromagnetic induction.

We have three major sources of energy to make electricity: coal, nuclear, and hydroelectricity (falling water). We boil water by using coal or nuclear energy and use the steam to turn a pinwheel (turbine), and connect the turbine to a generator. In the generator, the wire is moved through a magnetic field. The electric current is sent to our houses by wires. The third way to generate electricity is to have falling water spin the turbine. Very small amounts of electricity can also be produced by batteries and by solar cells.

In the United States, we get 33% of our energy from coal, 33% from natural gas, 1% from petroleum, or a total of 67% from fossil fuels. Nuclear power produces 20% percent of our energy needs. Hydropower provides 6% and renewables 7%. The largest portion of the renewables is generated by wind power.

Static electricity was discovered by a Greek man named Thales in about 600 BC. He found that when a piece of amber (the dried sap of a tree) was rubbed with cloth or fur, the charged amber attracted small objects.

Hans Christian Oersted discovered the relationship between electricity and magnetism in 1820. During a lecture Oersted accidentally laid a long wire near a compass needle. The wire was connected to a battery, and he noticed that the compass needle deflected.

## Q62: How does a hydrogen-powered car work?

There are a number of auto makers putting hydrogen-powered cars on the highway. The Hyundai Tucson is the latest. Honda has been testing their FCX fuel cell car and has put 43 in the hands of customers. Mercedes has leased a small fleet of hydrogen cars in California. Toyota now offers its Mirai model exclusively in California. California offers extremely generous rebates on alternative-fueled vehicles.

People are intrigued with hydrogen powered cars. And why not? Hydrogen is the most plentiful element in the universe. You can get hydrogen from ordinary water. Hydrogen and oxygen are obtained by applying a DC current to water in a process called electrolysis.

Using hydrogen has a huge advantage. The byproduct is water; no carbon emissions, no particles of nitrogen oxide, no smog, or air pollution.

Hydrogen also comes from natural gas. The process is expensive. And any natural gas used to make hydrogen is natural gas that is not available for power plants, industry, and home heating. There is no free lunch, no easy solutions.

The big problem with these cars is how to store the hydrogen fuel. If hydrogen is in gaseous form, it must be kept in tanks under extremely high pressure. The Daimler Chrysler Fuel Cell Car uses two under-floor tanks holding about three pounds of compressed hydrogen at 5,000 psi. Even so, drivers only get about 300 miles before they must fill up.

If hydrogen is in liquid form, it must be kept at a temperature of 420 degrees below zero Fahrenheit. This requires a giant thermos bottle. There are obvious problems with either method.

Research now centers on fixing hydrogen into a solid and using it as needed, much like the solid rocket fuel used by the military and NASA. However, at the present time, physicists have been able to make only a couple of atoms of solid hydrogen, at incredible pressure and very low temperature. There's a long way to go.

Hybrid cars have both an electric motor and a gasoline engine. But hydrogen cars are totally electric and are basically fuel cells. Fuel cells were used on the Apollo flights to the moon. Hydrogen and oxygen are mixed. Electricity and water are the reaction byproducts. You may recall that the Apollo 13 mission was aborted because one of the oxygen tanks blew up. The three-member crew barely made it back safely.

A fuel cell uses hydrogen and oxygen as the fuel. The fuel cell produces electricity and water. Hydrogen must be loaded on the car from a refueling station. The oxygen can be derived from air.

At the present time, there are very few places to fill up a car with hydrogen. A whole new infrastructure would have to be developed to manufacture, distribute, and sell hydrogen. There is a start. A total of $20 million per year has been set aside in California to develop such stations. Over forty are now in operation.

People are leery of using hydrogen. The German airship Hindenburg blew up on May 6, 1937 as it came in for a landing at Lakehurst, New Jersey. The Challenger Space Shuttle exploded on January 28, 1986 after taking off from Cape Kennedy. The shuttle utilized a large tank of liquid oxygen and a larger tank of liquid hydrogen.

A hydrogen gas bubble developed above the crippled nuclear reactor at Pennsylvania's Three Mile Island in 1979. When people hear the word hydrogen, they think of an explosion, even though an atom bomb type of explosion at Three Mile Island was not remotely possible.

These events, Hindenburg, Three Mile Island, Apollo 13, stick in people's mind. Young people who did not live through those times would certainly be reminded by the news media.

Despite the challenges with hydrogen fuel cells, a lot of progress has been made. The first hydrogen powered road vehicles were basically big trucks. Now companies are experimenting with car-sized vehicles. There may be a bright future for hydrogen cars, especially for urban fleets of cabs and buses.

Readers can purchase a toy hydrogen powered car for about $120.

## Q63: How do car alarms work?

A car gets stolen every 46 seconds in America. That's almost 700,000 cars per year. So car alarms are big business. The heart of any alarm system is a small computer that uses sensors to activate the alarms, which could be the horn, headlights, or an installed siren. The computer and alarms are powered by the car's battery, but some systems have an additional installed back-up battery. (Some thieves try clipping the battery cables).

The alarm sensors include simple switches, various pressure sensors, and motion detectors. The sensors activate when the doors, trunk, or hood open. Many of those switches operate like the one that makes the light come on in your refrigerator. The simplest alarm system is a switch on the door, wired so that if someone opened the door the siren starts wailing away. A more elaborate system has a radio receiver to allow wireless control from a key fob. A computer control unit, the brains of the system, monitors everything and sounds the alarm. Some systems have a valet switch, a manual shut-off, that disables the alarm system so that a valet can park your car. Some systems will sense a drop in voltage, indicating that someone is messing with the electrical system.

The first documented case of car theft in the United States was in 1895. Half of all stolen cars were left unlocked. The most frequently stolen vehicles today are the Honda Accord, Honda Civic, Ford F-Series Pickup, and the Chevrolet Full Size Pickup.

Police say that car owners should be able to furnish the following information in the event their car is missing; VIN (Vehicle Identification Number), year of car, make, model, color, and any unique features of the car, such as dents or bumper stickers.

## Q64: How do airbags activate?
. . . . . . . . . . . . . . . . . . . . . . . . . . .

Airbags have saved thousands of lives and allowed people to survive a crash that otherwise might have resulted in serious injury or death.

An airbag is a stretchable fabric that can be tightly packed into various locations in a vehicle and can be deployed in milliseconds as the bag fills with a gas to help cushion the driver and passengers. The most important part of the airbag is the crash sensor. A motorist wants the airbag to deploy in a crash, but not when he bumps into a car ahead while texting during a traffic jam!

The crash sensor responds to different inputs, the most important being a sudden stop. Other sensors measure wheel speed, seat occupant status, and brake pressure. Some sensors can activate seat belt locks and automatic door locks, in addition to airbag deployment.

There are two basic airbag sensors; electrical and mechanical. One common sensor is termed a "ball and tube," in which a ball is held by a small magnet. When a collision occurs, the ball is dislodged from the magnet, rolls forward in the tube, and hits a switch that activates the airbag.

Another popular and modern airbag sensor is the Micro Electro Mechanical Systems (MEMS) accelerometer, a small integrated circuit with internal micro-mechanical elements. The mechanical element moves in the case of a rapid stop, causing a change in capacitance that is detected by the electronics on the chip. The chip activates the airbag. Most autos have some sensors inside the car and some on the outside.

Once a sensor detects an actual crash, the next step is bag inflation. And it has to be fast, so fast that the driver's head doesn't smash into the steering wheel. The bag must be inflated with nitrogen gas within 55 milliseconds. A millisecond is one thousandth of a second.

The decision to deploy an airbag in a frontal crash is made within 15 to 30 milliseconds of the start of the crash. Airbags fully inflate within 75 milliseconds. The bag has to deploy at a speed of about 200 mph. If the deployment is too slow, the passengers risk injury from the airbag moving toward the passenger at the same time the passenger is moving toward the airbag.

Some manufacturers use an igniter pin that is driven into a sodium azide packet that produces the gas used to inflate the airbag. Then the bag has to deflate on its own once deployed. The gas escapes out tiny vent holes.

The automotive industry has warned drivers that the airbag can hurt a person who is out of position. That's why they preach that seatbelts must be worn if airbags are to be effective. Airbags are placed in the steering wheel for the driver and in the dashboard for the front passenger. That dashboard airbag on the passenger side is larger and therefore more expensive than the driver's airbag. Side doors also hide airbags. Modern cars can wrap a person in a cocoon of airbags.

Deployed airbags have been known to kill kids in the front seat. Most states have rules regulating when kids may ride in the front seat. Guidelines are based on age and weight.

Airbags have been used by spacecraft landing on Mars, the F-111 fighter/bomber, and the Army's Blackhawk and Kiowa Warrior helicopter.

Mercedes-Benz was the first to install airbags, starting in 1980. A poignant milestone occurred in April, 1990. Two cars, both Chrysler LeBarons, both equipped with airbags, collided head-on at Culpeper, Virginia. The estimated combined speed was 70 mph. One car strayed over the centerline initiating the crash. One driver had a cut on his elbow and a bruised knee. The other driver suffered a bloody nose and minor bruises. Both walked away. The press headlined the accident as "dueling airbags."

## Q65: Does a fast jet plane burn as much fuel when it goes slowly?

. . . . . . . . . . . . . . . . . . . . . . . . . . . . . . . . . . . . . . . . . . . . .

A good question and a very complex one! The answer is simple for cars, but not for planes. For cars, fuel efficiency is greatest when you're running the engine at the lowest speed in the highest gear possible. Anytime you push that accelerator, the gas mileage goes down, regardless of car size and type.

As for jet planes, all jet engines are reaction engines. They take air in the front and mix it with jet fuel (high grade kerosene) that burns and expels the gases out the back at high speed. It's a beautiful example of Newton's Third Law of Action-Reaction.

There are several different types of jet engines: turbojets, turbofans, ramjets, and pulse jets. The most common type on passenger jet planes are the high-bypass turbofan engines. They give high speed over long distances with excellent fuel efficiency.

Jet engines have both a propulsive efficiency and cycle efficiency. The propulsive efficiency is highest when the gases coming out the back of the engine match the speed of the plane forward.

The cycle efficiency has to do with the temperature of the gases shooting out the back. The higher the temperature, the greater the efficiency. Efficiency decreases with increasing speed, but greater distances are covered with greater plane speed.

It turns out that efficiency per mile, which is what we really care about, is not dependent on the speed of the plane. However, airplane bodies (airframes) are not efficient at supersonic speeds. They are too big and too wide.

That's why all the planes we fly on travel below the speed of sound, which is about 750 miles per hour. Most fly at about 560 mph. An exception was the British-French SST Concorde that flew at about twice the speed of sound. When you look at the Concorde, or a picture of it, you see that it is shaped like a jet fighter, very narrow and quite long. It could only carry 100 passengers and a crew of nine. It had four big thirsty noisy Rolls Royce engines. Traveling over land, it had to slow down to half speed because of the sonic boom in its wake. No need to rattle Grandma's dishes in the cupboard or cause chickens and turkeys to bunch up and die.

One Air France Concorde crashed in July, 2000 with loss of all 109 passengers and crew on board and four people on the ground. The Concorde was taken out of service in 2003. The owners cited a slump in air travel following 9/11, high maintenance costs, outdated instrumentation, high ticket costs, low seating capacity, and possible compromise of the ozone layer.

One of the most efficient means of air travel is the turboprop. You may see four-engine C-130 cargo planes around military bases. It is a gas turbine engine that also turns a geared-down propeller. Propeller aircraft are most efficient at low altitude, where the air is thicker. Jets are more efficient at higher altitudes where the air is thinner and propellers can't operate.

Commuter airlines use a lot of these turboprop aircraft. When some passengers see that propeller, they worry that these planes are not as safe as jet planes. Accident statistics indicate that turboprops have as good if not better safety record than pure jets. But perception is often more powerful than reality, so in the last few decades commuter airlines have phased out propeller-driven aircraft and purchased jet aircraft.

## Q66: Where is the black box carried on an airplane?

Those data recording black boxes are actually painted orange so they'll show up well in any wreckage. There are usually two of them and they are stored in the tail of the airplane. Storage back there in the tail improves their chances of surviving a crash. Did you ever hear of an airplane backing into a mountain? It just doesn't happen.

The casing of a black box consists of two shells of stainless steel with a heat-protective material between the shells. The case must withstand a temperature of two thousand degrees Fahrenheit for thirty minutes.

Inside the case, on shockproof mounts, are the plane's flight data and cockpit voice recorders. The flight data recorder is continually fed information on the speed, direction, altitude, acceleration, engine thrust, engine performance, and position of the flight controls. There are a total of about a hundred different parameters. The data are recorded on stainless steel tape which has the thickness of aluminum foil. When the tape is played back, it generates a computer printout.

The cockpit voice recorder records the previous thirty minutes of the crew's conversation and radio transmissions. This is a continuous loop tape, so only the last thirty minutes are saved.

New planes joining the airline fleets use solid-state recorders, essentially stacked arrays of computer chip boards about two inches by one inch. No moving parts means greater reliability, less maintenance, and less chance of anything breaking in a crash. These newer units record 25 hours of flight data and two hours of cockpit conversations. Up to 700 sets of data can be recorded.

The cockpit voice recorder has four microphones; one in the pilot's headset, one in the co-pilot's (first officer) headset, one in the third crewmember's headset, and one mounted in the center of the cockpit, so it can pick up alerts and alarms.

Black boxes are also equipped with an underwater locator beacon. If the plane crashes into water, the beacon sends out an ultrasonic pulse that can be detected by sonar and acoustical locating equipment. A sensor is activated when touched by water. It pings once per second for thirty days.

Air France Flight 447 from Rio de Janeiro to Paris, a wide body Airbus A330, crashed into the Atlantic Ocean in June, 2009, killing all 228 people abroad. It took nearly two years to find the black boxes in deep water. It required an advanced robotic submersible and millions of dollars to find and retrieve the black boxes.

So now the thinking has changed. Why not stream the data in real time to either satellites or ground stations? The technology already exists. Anyone with a smart phone can receive streaming data from the stock markets.

The Canadian airplane maker, Bombardier, announced recently that their jets will transmit telemetry data in real time, as well as record it the traditional way on black boxes.

A recent patent, called Safelander, would enable a ground-based pilot to take remote control of an airplane in flight. The Safelander system might have foiled the 9/11 hijackers if it had been in place. The military routinely flies drones in surveillance and combat missions. There are now discussions about cargo-only aircraft, such as United Parcel and Fed Ex, being flown by remote control, with no cockpit crew whatsoever. We are living in truly exciting and wondrous times!

## Q67: What happened to the Mars Polar Lander?

NASA has experienced six decades of spectacular space exploration. Stunning successes culminated in the Apollo moon landing in 1969. There have been rare failures. In 1999, NASA lost a spacecraft. It was the $165 million Mars Polar Lander launched on Jan 3, 1999 and expected to land near the South Pole of Mars on Dec 3, 1999. The Mars Polar Lander did not phone home. The spacecraft was supposed to search for water, slam two probes into the surface, and use a microphone to listen for the sounds of Mars.

A NASA team used detective work and post-crash testing and analysis to try and figure out what went wrong. Since there was no telemetry capability from the MPL during atmospheric entry, descent, or landing, there can be no way to know for sure exactly what happened. While a number of failure scenarios were examined, a specific candidate failure scenario emerged—one borne out by repeated ground-based, post-failure testing.

Four tests in early 2000 by Lockheed Martin in Denver showed that sensors in the MPL's landing gear sent out spurious (false) signals. Software that should have been designed to ignore these signals was not designed to do so after all. These signals were interpreted by the spacecraft as indicating the forces landing legs would experience upon landing. The onboard computers received signals that the spacecraft had touched the surface of Mars.

As a result, the descent engines were shut off. This design flaw was not caught before launch since a series of tests used sensors that were wired incorrectly. Ergo, the problem was not detected, and the Mars Polar Lander was sent on a doomed flight to Mars. Still, there is no way to be certain that this flaw was the actual cause of the MPL failure.

What are we to make of this failure? The news media reports only glorious successes and glaring downfalls. But real lab science involves many setbacks along with some progress. Failures are common in any scientific research. Failure is how you make progress. You learn by making mistakes. Just look at all the failures to cure the common cold or find a vaccine for AIDS. And what about the $165 million bucks spent on the failed mission? Well, all that money was spent here on Earth, in the good old USA, going into salaries and materials. It did not go overseas to build a swimming pool for some two-bit dictator.

Some people would argue that basic research is seldom a

waste of money. Remember that 'Star Wars' program started during the Reagan administration to shoot down incoming enemy missiles? Just the other day, it was reported that a downsized laser developed for Star Wars destroyed a deep-seated brain tumor in a woman patient. You never really know where research will lead.

Earthlings will go on exploring Mars, sending spacecraft, probes, and then supplies. Man will follow. At one time there was water on Mars. We can see the dried-up channels where water flowed. What happened to it, and can it happen on Earth? What are the dynamics of vast climate changes over millions of years? There have been successful journeys by spacecraft to all the planets in our solar system. There were some failures in the past and there will be again in the future. That's how science works!!

What about successes? NASA launched the Mars Exploration Rover named Spirit in 2003. It landed in 2004. It operated for 6 years beyond its planned usefulness, and got stuck in sand. NASA gave up on Spirit in 2011.

Another Rover, Opportunity, was launched in 2003, landed in 2004, and is currently working perfectly and sending back info on a regular basis. Curiosity was launched in 2011, landed in 2012, and is still operational. NASA has an exemplary record of Mars exploration.

## Q68: What are rockets used for besides going into space?

We are all quite aware that rockets are used to launch spaceships into Earth orbit and to visit other planets. We use rockets for weather satellites, communications satellites, spy satellites, Earth resources and navigation (GPS) satellites, and for getting to the International Space Station.

Historically, rockets were used in warfare. The Chinese made gunpowder rockets in 1232 AD. These "fire arrows" were designed to hold off the "Mongol hordes" in warfare. Later, the Mongol chieftain, Genghis Khan, used similar rockets to help conquer much of Asia and Eastern Europe.

The British, with rockets developed by William Congreve, bombarded Fort McHenry outside of Baltimore in 1814. That bombardment inspired Francis Scott Key's "rockets' red glare" in the Star-Spangled Banner.

Konstantin Tsiolkovsky in Russia and Robert Goddard in the United States made huge strides in rocket technology, especially in fuels, combustion chambers, and high-speed pumps.

The Germans developed the V-2 rockets with a one-ton bomb on top. Over 3,000 rained down on London during WWII, and some on Antwerp.

JATO (Jet Assisted Take-Off) and RATO (Rocket Assisted Take-Off), were used to get heavy aircraft off short runways or aircraft carrier decks. Early jet engines did not have much thrust at low speeds. Rockets have also been used to shoot equipment from shore into the water to rescue sailors.

Fireworks employ a rocket to take them up several hundred feet, where a time-delay fuse activates the charge that gives us that familiar air burst. The fireworks' rocket engine fuel is gunpowder, a mixture of 75 percent potassium nitrate, 15 percent charcoal, and 10 percent sulfur. Using big rockets like the Saturn that took men to the Moon does have some drawbacks. Lots of fuel is used, and the rocket punches a hole in the ozone layer. We need the ozone to protect us from ultraviolet radiation. Chemical rockets are not efficient. It takes about 15 pounds of fuel to put one pound of spacecraft into Earth orbit.

A jet engine carries fuel but uses the oxygen in the air for combustion. A rocket has to carry both the fuel and oxygen it will use.

Today, private space flight companies are providing the excitement, not NASA. SpaceShipTwo, a spacecraft carried aloft by a White Knight Two carrier airplane, is expected to fly people into space soon.

No fewer than ten companies are vying for the space business. Orbital Science Corporation secured a $1.9 billion contract to fly eight cargo missions to the International Space Station. Private companies such as SpaceX are already contracted to take supplies to the International Space Station. Space X founder Elon Musk claims that his company will send astronauts to space at a price of $20 million each. Lockheed Martin, Boeing, Sierra Nevada Space Systems, and Blue Origin are carving out their own niches in the space business.

Space travel is expensive now, but in a few years, people of modest means will be able to buy a ticket to get into Earth orbit, about 150 miles high, take ninety minutes for an orbit, and land on a runway. The price of the ticket will probably depend on how many orbits you want. Space tourism is not far away.

## Q69: How does a quartz watch work?

The heart of a quartz watch is a tiny slice of crystal or ceramic material. Certain crystals will produce a small voltage when flexed. This effect is termed piezoelectricity, from the Greek word 'to press'. The atoms in these crystals are held tightly together by their electric charges.

Quartz has positive silicon and negative oxygen ions (charged particles). If you press on the crystal, the negative ions move to one side of the crystal and the positive ions move to the other side. You can get a big discharge or spark from such a crystal. Most gas grills are ignited by piezoelectric starters.

The reverse also happens. If you apply a voltage to such a crystal, it will flex or vibrate at a precise natural rate or frequency. This is called a quartz oscillator. The quartz oscillator is the heart of a quartz watch.

Energy or power from a battery or solar cell makes a crystal vibrate, and it gives out voltage pulses that are sent to a microchip. The microchip changes this rate to one pulse per second. This signal then turns the hands of the watch or activates a digital display.

Quartz watches use a tiny bar quartz crystal that vibrates at a rate of 32 kilohertz (KHz). That is 32,000 vibrations per second. Circuitry divides that number down to a few pulses per second to drive an LCD (liquid crystal display) or to drive the gears of the traditional mechanical hands. The LCD is the kind we see on most hand calculators, with black numbers on gray background.

Quartz watches came out in the early 1970's. They had a red LED read-out and cost about $500. The price has fallen dramatically, so that very good quartz watches are given away with McDonald's kids meals.

Try this simple science experiment. Simulate the natural vibration frequency of a quartz watch by using a water balloon in a bowl or pan. Inflate a balloon with water. Knot or tie off the nozzle of the balloon. Place the water balloon in a bowl or pan that is slightly too small to hold the balloon. Gently rap or tap on the water balloon. Note that the water balloon will vibrate at a fixed rate for several seconds.

## Q70: *What makes the face on my wristwatch glow in the dark?*

. . . . . . . . . . . . . . . . . . . . . . . . . . . . . . . . . . . . . . .

Good thing you have a newer watch. Some of those old "glow-in-the-dark" wristwatches used radium, which is highly radioactive. Today watchmakers use two common approaches to allow you to read your watch in the dark.

TimexTM watches glow in the dark when you push a button. They use zinc sulfide mixed with copper. A tiny microchip applies a voltage to the zinc sulfide. This voltage excites the zinc sulfide atoms.

Electrons move to orbits further away from the nucleus. When the voltage is turned off, the electrons fall back to their original orbits, and the atoms release light. The most efficient material and color combinations glow green.

The same technology works in the "glow-in-the-dark" pens that came out in the 1950's. Kids use glow-in-the-dark materials to put stars on their bedroom ceiling. Soldiers use strips of it on helmets. Photographers put it on their chemical bottles so they can read the labels in the dark.

The atoms in these materials are not excited by electricity, but rather by ultraviolet light from sunlight, fluorescent light or incandescent light.

Some glow-in-the-dark wristwatches utilize radioactive tritium gas sealed in a tube. The tritium gas emits beta particles which strike phosphors that coat the glass tube. These watches will glow for about 25 years, and unlike the Timex watches, do not need a power source.

Tritium-powered watches are considered safe and have passed all government regulations. In the worse-case scenario, if a capsule breaks, the tritium, being a gas, disperses harmlessly in the air.

## Q71: *What is an atomic clock?*
. . . . . . . . . . . . . . . . . . . . . . . . . .

When you buy a clock labeled "atomic clock" you are buying one that can be synchronized to the United States official atomic clock in Colorado. These clocks and wristwatches can pick up the radio transmissions of broadcast stations on several frequencies.

The National Institute of Standards and Technology (NIST) airs time signals from powerful transmitters on two radio stations: WWV from Fort Collins, Colorado and WWVH from Kauai, Hawaii. The frequencies are 2.5, 5, 10, 15, and 20 MHz. Reception of any radio signal can be affected by weather, terrain, location, time of day, time of year, and atmospheric and ionosphere conditions. Using so many frequencies insures reception anywhere in the world for at least part of the day.

A grandfather clock keeps time by the steady back and forth oscillations of a pendulum. The pendulum is powered by falling weights. Old-time clocks use a balance wheel alternating backward and forward. Power is provided by a wound spring. Quartz watches depend on the vibrating oscillations of a crystal. Power is furnished by a battery.

Atomic clocks, the kind used by NIST, go back to 1945 when physicist Isidor Rabi determined that atoms maintain a steady unchanging vibration rate, more precise than the pendulum, balance wheel, or quartz crystal. Early atomic clocks used the vibration of ammonia molecules, but today's atomic clocks go with cesium.

The radio receiver for an atomic clock is tiny, about the size of a pencil tip. It can easily be embedded in computer chips and it can be utilized in GPS units and cell phones. The miniature receiver needs only to pick up the radio transmission once each few days to correct any error in the receiver's clock. Generally, the clock updates at night when the signal is strongest.

WWV sends a digital time code on 60 KHz that modulates or changes the power of the carrier signal picked up by the receiving antenna. The receiver decodes the bits to get the time, the day of the year, daylight saving time, and leap year indicators. The final output is called the Coordinated Universal Time.

Estimates vary as to the accuracy of an atomic clock. One scientist claims precision to within one second in 126 years. Another report puts it at one second in 30 million years. Either one will get you to the church on time!

Many home automation devices, including computers connected to the Internet, are continually and automatically updated to the correct time.

The NIST has the big expensive atomic clocks that generate extremely accurate time signals and you and I can buy inexpensive atomic clocks that are synchronized to the government atomic clocks.

Listen in on WWV on any one of the frequencies listed above or any short-wave radio receiver. The 15 and 20 MHZ signals are strongest during the day. The 5 MHz and 10 MHz come in best at night. You hear the steady tick, tick, tick, and then a human voice announces the time on the minute. It's quite amazing!

# Chapter Eight

# At the Fringes
## of Science

## Q72: *What is the God particle?*
· · · · · · · · · · · · · · · · · · · · · · · · · · ·

The "God particle" is the label of a subatomic particle called the Higgs boson. Different subatomic particles are responsible for giving matter different properties. One of the most mysterious and important properties is mass.

Some particles, like protons, neutrons, and electrons have mass. Others, like photons, do not have mass. The Higgs boson, or "God particle," is believed to be the particle which gives mass to matter. The Higgs boson took thousands of scientists nearly five decades to discover at an estimated cost of $13.25 billion.

The "God particle" nickname came from the 1993 book *The God Particle: If the Universe Is the Answer, What Is the Question?* by Leon Lederman. Since then, the name has taken on a life of its own, in part because of the monumental questions about matter that the God particle might be able to answer.

The Higgs particle was hypothesized back in the 1960s by British physicist Peter Higgs and others to fill a weird gap in the Standard Model, one of physics' most successful theories.

The Standard Model of particle physics is a system that attempts to identify the basic particles that make up matter. The Standard Model is still a very good method of understanding particle physics, and it continues to improve. The Model predicts that there are certain elementary particles even smaller than protons and neutrons.

Peter Higgs, a British theoretical physicist, proposed a particle in the 1960s to "fill in the gaps" in the Standard Model. If we could find the particle, Higgs said, it should answer many very hard questions about why there is something rather than nothing.

For decades, the Higgs boson was the holy grail of particle physics. Without the Higgs boson and Higgs field, nothing would exist—no animals, oceans, planets or stars.

For more than four decades, physicists assumed that the Higgs particle existed, but found no experimental evidence for it.

It required a super-powerful particle smasher such as the Large Hadron Collider to produce energies high enough to knock a Higgs boson into existence under controlled conditions.

Confirmation of the existence of the Higgs particle came in March of 2013 at the Large Hadron Collider at CERN (Conseil Européen pour la Recherche Nucléaire) in Geneva, Switzerland.

Protons are present in the nuclei of atoms, the basic units of mater. Protons are composed of even smaller particles: three quarks held together by gluons. Scientists smash protons together by accelerating them at 99.9999991 percent of the speed of light in a 16.8-mile-long underground ringed tunnel.

Quarks and gluons inside the protons collide and explode with enough energy to create the Higgs particle. The Higgs particle lasts less than a millionth of a billionth of a billionth of a second before decaying into a spray of other particles. Evidence of the Higgs particle was found in the spirals and streaks left in the Large Hadron Collider detectors as it disintegrates.

Peter Higgs is not thrilled by the nickname "God particle," as he is an avowed atheist. There isn't really any religious intention behind the nickname. Higgs, born in 1929, earned the Nobel Prize in Physics in 2013 for his successful prediction.

## Q73: *What is a jackalope?*

A jackalope is an imaginary animal that is supposed to be a cross between a jack rabbit and a pronghorn antelope.

Where did this good-hearted foolishness start? It all began in a 1930s hunting trip for jackrabbits near Douglas, Wyoming. Douglas Herrick and his brother invited a bunch of hunters from out East for a visit. Several days after the hunt, Douglas Herrick looked in a bin of jackrabbit remains and deer antlers, and the idea was born. Why not mount a set of antlers on top of a rabbit? After all, the Herrick brothers had studied taxidermy by mail order as kids. They sold the first jackalope for ten dollars. The *New York Times* wrote a story about this mythical creature. The legend spread.

Douglas, Wyoming has been named the "Home of the Jackalope." A large statue of a jackalope stands in the town square of Douglas, Wyoming, population of about 5,000. The jackalope adorns Douglas's city fire trucks and park benches. You can buy a season Jackalope Hunting License from the Douglas Chamber of Commerce for ten dollars. It is good for only one day of the year, June 31. Do keep in mind that June has only thirty days!! Also, the purchasing hunter may not have an IQ greater than 72.

The House side of the Wyoming state legislature passed a bill, by a vote of 45-12, in 2005, naming the jackalope the "official mythological creature" of Wyoming. The bill was indefinitely postponed in the State Senate on March 2, 2005. Those Wyoming folks do have a sense of humor!

Wall Drug in Wall, S.D. has a large jackalope statue. This seven-foot jackalope comes with a saddle, and tourists are encouraged to have their picture taken astride the giant beast. A minor-league hockey team in Texas is named the Odessa Jackalopes.

President Ronald Reagan had a jackalope mounted on the wall of his California ranch, Rancho del Cielo, near Santa Barbara in the Santa Ynez Mountain range. Reagan claimed he caught the brute himself.

The jackalope joins a long line of fairy-tale creatures such as the Loch Ness monster, Big Foot, King Kong, vampires, dragons, centaurs, mermaids, and unicorns.

## Q74: *Is time travel possible?*
. . . . . . . . . . . . . . . . . . . . . . .

You want to time travel into the future? That is theoretically possible. Want to travel back in time? No such luck, definitely not possible!

When scientists start looking at time travel, the math gets very complicated. Oh, it's easy in science fiction. The big hero can step into a machine, push a button, and travel forward in time or backward in time.

Time travel involves wormholes, event horizons, geodesics, and worldlines. There is nothing in Einstein's Theory of General Relativity that will prevent time travel into the future. Time travel to the future doesn't violate the principles of causality.

Causality says that one thing causes another thing to happen. If you kick a soccer ball, the cause of you accelerating the ball with your foot has the effect of the ball flying out across the soccer field. The reverse can't happen. The ball can't come back from the field and cause your foot to accelerate it. That would be going backward in time. Going "Back to the Future" is a contradiction.

However, there is no problem for causality if you kick the ball, and then immediately travel forward in time to the point where the ball has been lying in the grass for a week. You picking up the ball would come after the cause of you kicking the ball out into the soccer field.

In 1935, Albert Einstein and Nathan Rosen used the theory of general relativity to propose the existence of "bridges" through space and time. These bridges, or wormholes, connect two different points in space. Space and time are tangled to form something called the space-time continuum.

A wormhole can be thought of as a shortcut through the space-time continuum, like a tunnel. But there is the danger of a sudden collapse, high radiation, and contact with exotic matter.

Certain solutions of general relativity allow for the existence of wormholes where the mouth of each is a black hole. However, a naturally occurring black hole, formed by the collapse of a dying star, does not by itself create a wormhole.

All this talk about finding wormholes and traveling through time is very speculative. It is not something that is going to happen soon, if ever.

Speaking of time, did you ever try to define time? It's not easy. Author Elbert Hubbard (1856-1915) said, "Time is one damn thing after another." Historian Arnold Toynbee described history in the same terms, "one damn thing after another."

American physicist John Archibald Wheeler (1911-2008), who was a collaborator with Albert Einstein, offered that "time is what keeps everything from happening at once."

The speed of light is about 186,000 miles per second. Thus far, the fastest humans have traveled is 5 miles per second when astronauts were going to and coming back from the moon.

The faster one travels, the slower time moves relative to the stationary observer.

Sirius, the Dog Star and brightest star we see in the night sky, is about nine light years away. If you traveled at 99.99999999 percent of the speed of light, you could go set off for Sirius in the morning and get back late at night. You would be less than a day older, but everyone else on Earth would have aged by eighteen years. There is no magic here, no voodoo of any sort. However, there is a problem with humans trying to go that fast. We have no way at the present time of getting to those speeds.

Actually, a telescope is a kind of time machine. It allows you to look into the past. If you see the Andromeda Galaxy in the night sky, you are looking 2 million years into the past. The light that you see tonight left Andromeda 2 million years ago. The

Andromeda Galaxy may not even be out there anymore. All we know is how it looked 2 million years ago.

You can't see or look into the future because it hasn't happened yet. We can make predictions and conjectures about the future. Most of those guesses are predicated on what we already know.

All of us should care about the future, because we will spend the rest of our lives there!

## Q75: Is Bigfoot real?

No. There is no Bigfoot, sasquatch, or yeti. Bigfoot is a big hoax! Oh, there are some famous pictures and videos of Bigfoot. The 1967 video shot by Roger Patterson and Bob Gimlin in the woods in northern California is impressive. Impressive until you learn they admitted that one of them dressed up in a bear/monkey suit while the other shot the film. Then they went to a tavern for a few brews and even showed their monkey suit outfit, thrown in the trunk of their car, to a few friends. But wouldn't you know it, because even after being thoroughly discredited, the film still runs on television.

Raymond L. Wallace claimed to have started the modern Bigfoot phenomenon in 1958. He used phony foot casts to leave Bigfoot prints in California. His brother, Wilbur L. Wallace, later admitted the hoax and showed the wooden "feet" that were used to delude an eager public.

The pictures we see of Bigfoot are basically unsubstantiated folklore and hoaxes, designed to sell tabloids, books, and television programs. There is no proof that any such creature lived or is living. There is a distinct lack of bones or a body, just fuzzy photographs and jittery video.

There are suggestions that people may have mistaken bears for Bigfoot, as alleged sightings often occur near habitats of bears. Bears, especially grizzlies, are large and furry and often stand up on their hind legs. This has led to speculation that Bigfoot witnesses mistook bears for something more exotic.

Quite frankly, I am not big on conspiracy theories or paranormal stuff. Bruno Hauptmann did kidnap and murder the Lindbergh baby in 1932. Julius and Ethel Rosenberg did conspire to sell atomic bomb secrets to the Soviets. Lee Harvey Oswald acted alone when he killed President Kennedy in 1963. Yes, O.J Simpson most likely killed Nicole Brown Simpson and Ronald Goldman in June 1994. No, UFOs from outer space have never visited us, not even in Area 51 in Nevada or Roswell, New Mexico. The Loch Ness monster does not exist, but it does draw tourists to Scotland. Carl Sagan, astronomer, writer, and television science producer often stated that the universe is beautiful and knowable. He talked about Occam's Razor, a principle that states that the explanation of any phenomenon should make as few assumptions as possible. The simplest explanation for any phenomenon usually is the correct one.

Occam was the 14th century Franciscan friar William of Ockham. Ockham is in the county of Surrey in England, just a bit southwest of London.

### Q76: Do divining rods or dowsing actually find water or underground pipes?
. . . . . . . . . . . . . . . . . . . . . . . . . . . . . . . . . . . . . . . . . . . .

No. That's my answer and I'm sticking to it! Yes, dowsing is controversial and has many ardent adherents. There are people who will swear on a stack of Bibles that they have used water witching and dowsing or have witnessed finding water or underground pipes or wires. But controlled tests and studies over many decades yielded results no better than chance.

Dowsing is the art of finding hidden things with aid of dowsing sticks, rods, or a pendulum. A forked stick, a small Y-shaped willow branch, is most often used. The dowser holds the branch by the ends of the Y-shaped branch with the stem end pointed straight ahead and parallel to the ground. The dowser begins to walk over the specified area. When the end of the branch is suddenly and violently drawn downward, the dowser says "Dig here for water."

Other dowsers will use two L-shaped metal rods, one in each hand. The short arms are held upright and free to swivel, and the long arm points forward. When something is discovered, the rods cross over one another making an X over the found object. Some dowsers specify brass rods, others use metal coat hangers.

Water can be found anywhere you drill. There is no way to confirm that the spot chosen by the dowser is the best possible spot.

The first bona-fide study of dowsing was done in 1948, and not a single dowser had results any better than random luck. A German study in 1987 tested 500 dowsers and selected the best 43 for further testing. The vast number showed no results in excess of arbitrary or hit-and-miss guesses.

A controlled experiment in Maine in 1949 was run by the American Society for Psychical Research. A group of 27 dowsers "failed completely to estimate the depth or amount of water to be found in a field free of surface clues for water, whereas a geologist and engineer successfully predicted the depth at which water would be found in sixteen sites in the same field."

Some dowsers make claims of a psychic connection. They will speak of an energy force. They say they're able to tune in to the vibration of an object. The dowsing twig or tool acts as an amplifier or antenna for tuning into this secret energy source.

Dowsing belongs in the same category as psychics, the Loch Ness monster, Yeti, the Abominable Snowman, Bigfoot, the Bermuda Triangle, visits by UFOs and aliens, ghosts, haunted houses, ESP, astrology, predictions by Jeanne Dixon, John Edwards and Sylvia Brown, and the Grassy Knoll theory. All possible, but not probable, and there is no evidence or proof that any exist.

Religion has weighed in on the subject. Martin Luther, in 1518, put dowsing for metals in the same category as occultism. The Jesuit, Gaspar Schott, declared dowsing to be "superstitious, or rather satanic," in 1662.

Most people, it seems, just enjoy watching a dowser at work and don't imagine any religious connotation or connection. It is entertaining to see when a branch dips down or metal rods cross.

## Q77: What are some big misconceptions about science?

There are several worth noting. First, science doesn't explain everything. Science means making connections to things we already know. Science is not a matter of collecting isolated facts. We understand how rainbows form in the sky after we know how light goes through a prism. We grasp lightning in the sky when we shuffle across a rug and get a spark as we touch a doorknob. Science is an exciting, dynamic process for discovering how the world works.

Science doesn't always make sense. Does it make sense that sunlight is actually made up of six or seven colors? That everything we see forms an upside-down image in our eye? That the sun is almost a million miles wide? Science causes disbelief, bewilderment, and wonder. But that is how we learn and construct knowledge.

Science cares about questions more than answers. Students think that science teachers should have all the answers. Far from it! It is amazing that scientists themselves will admit that they know very little. Einstein asked very simple questions. Why is the sky blue? Why is the Earth round? What makes a magnet work? Answers lead to new questions. The richer the question that is asked the richer the results. There is not a single scientific method. The process of science is complex and unpredictable.

Scientists have a lot of fun. They like to fool around, but they call it experimenting. Sometimes scientists have big and/or expensive toys. They like trial and error stuff. They see something that looks interesting and they go after it. Science is one of the most creative activities that humans can engage in.

Science and technology can't solve all our problems. Science has conquered many dreadful diseases, built things that make our life easier and more comfortable, and helped us communicate with people all over the world. Science can't control people's beliefs, emotions, or behavior. It is the decisions and choices that people make that lead to many problems. In that respect, science is quite limited.

## Q78: Are there questions science can't answer?

Yes, there are plenty of questions that stymie science. Around 1900, the most famous scientist in the world was Lord Kelvin. William Thomson was his real name, and he made huge advances in electricity and the study of heat. He made the comment, "There is nothing new to be discovered in physics." That was before airplanes, atomic energy, computers, and space exploration.

It would be more accurate if Lord Thomson had said, "Rather than having waded deep into the sea of knowledge, we have merely dipped our toes in the water."

There are mysteries that may remain unsolved. The Grand Theory of Everything, trying to combine the four known forces of physics (electricity, gravity, and the strong and weak nuclear forces) into one unifying theory, has been an elusive goal of science.

The works of Newton and Darwin were comprehensible to most literate people. But the strange world of modern science is so surreal and counterintuitive that it leaves most of us baffled. Things like time-space stretching like a rubber membrane, gravitational wormholes that allow one to go faster than the speed of light, string theory, and quantum mechanics—these notions are far removed from the everyday world in which we live.

The nature of time is a mystery. Plato thought that time was an illusion. Einstein said that clocks run slower the faster you go. Nobel Prize scientist and builder of the atomic bomb John Wheeler claimed that "Time is nature's way to keep everything from happening at once."

A frequent question on youngster's minds is why people die. It's a good question and one for which science does not have a very good answer. Even though death is not very popular, no one has come up with a surefire way to extent life beyond about a hundred years.

Here are a few condensed versions from those who are supposed to know why we die: the body just wears out, we are genetically programmed to age and die, and ageing is a process which makes us increasingly vulnerable to various diseases.

Of course, we know there are ways of increasing the chances that we will live longer. We can avoid smoking and follow a sensible diet. We can avoid risky behavior, such as not wearing seatbelts and motorcycle helmets. We can stay away as much as possible from all those chemical additives in our foods, cleaning products, cosmetics, lawns, etc.

But, in the final analysis, why we die is a mystery for which science offers no reasonable answer.

How did the universe begin? There is overwhelming evidence for the Big Bang Theory, but no one knows how it started. How life began is also a mystery. Science does not have a definitive answer. Are we alone in the universe? Most scientists would say the universe is probably teeming with life, but we don't have any proof. Their speculation is based on probabilities.

How does the human mind work? Scientists are scratching their heads on this question (no pun intended). Intriguing breakthroughs are being made in neuroscience and brain chemistry. Why do we need sleep? There are a handful of proposed explanations, but no general agreement. Can science produce computer technology to replace damaged brain cells? When can we expect cures for cancers and heart disease?

Here's another puzzling mystery: What is the universe made of? You may have heard of dark matter and dark energy. Supposedly, we can only see five percent of the universe. Roughly 68 percent of the Universe is dark energy and 27 percent is dark matter. Now that is a real unknown! So, yes, there are plenty of questions science has not yet been able to answer.

## Q79: What is meant by the sixth dimension, and how does it connect to black holes?

Modern science is composed of two seemingly incompatible theories. One theory, general relativity, championed by Albert Einstein, explains how big things work, like planets and galaxies. The other theory, quantum mechanics, successfully explains the workings of things that are very small, like atoms and subatomic particles. There is a lot of incompatibility between these two theories.

Einstein's Theory of Relativity is really an extension of Isaac Newton's concept of how the world works. All the laws of mass, energy, and motion that you and I experience in everyday life are explained by Newton's Three Laws. Albert Einstein extended Newton's Laws to things that move very fast, close to the speed of light.

Einstein tried to find a single theory that would embrace all of nature's laws: a single theory that would marry relativity, used on the astronomical level, to quantum mechanics, used at the atomic level. Einstein spent forty years trying, but was not successful. Discovering a single unifying theory, a single master equation, is today's Holy Grail of science.

Today, cutting-edge talk in physics is all about something called "string theory," sometimes referred to as the "Theory of Everything." String theory scientists discuss eleven dimensions and parallel universes. Strings are tiny bits of energy, vibrating like strings on a guitar.

The first three dimensions are length, width, and depth. It required three numbers to pinpoint our physical location at any given moment. Slap a time stamp on those coordinates, and a person is pinpointed in time as well. Could there be a fourth or fifth dimension? Some scientists have speculated and discussed a space-time dimension. In 1919, mathematician Theodor Kaluza theorized that a fourth dimension might link general relativity and electromagnetism. There is something out there called string theory with a proposed 10 or 11 dimensions. All of this talk of a multi-dimensioned universe is highly speculative.

Six-dimensional space has six degrees of freedom and uses six coordinates or points to specify a location in space. Three of these dimensions are translational along an x, y, and z coordinates, and the other three are sets of rotations.

There does happen to be a real-life example of six dimensions. NASA has a spacesuit that an astronaut could fit into to operate outside the space shuttle. This Manned Maneuvering Unit (MMU) allows an astronaut to move in all axis or degrees of freedom; side to side, right to left, up and down, pitch, roll, and yaw. The astronaut is said to move in all six dimensions.

No one really knows how many dimensions make up the universe. It is a very exciting field of research. Black holes may provide clues to aid astronomers in thinking about many dimensions. The extremely strong gravitational field of a black hole complicates the issue. Inside a black hole, time becomes a dimension, giving rise to the fourth-dimensional term "space-time."

We're never really sure what will be the outcome of all this research. In the 1920s, there was lots of speculation on the value of quantum mechanics. "What good is it?" people asked. It turns out that all modern electronics, smart phones, flat screen television, GPS, lasers, microcircuits, LED's, came about because of the research used in quantum theory.

## Q80: What is the Turing Test?

During World War II, the Germans had a top-secret code machine called Enigma. Enigma looked like a typewriter in a wooden box, with rotors that turned on spindles. One or more of those rotors would turn each time a key was pressed.

Most of the German military message traffic was encrypted on the Enigma machines. The Germans considered the Enigma code to be unbreakable. The British set up a 55-acre estate outside of London, called Bletchley Park, to prove them wrong.

The intelligence produced by breaking the German code was termed "Ultra."

Ultra helped the British and Americans decipher virtually all the Germans' troop movements, U-boat strategies, and aircraft movements during the war. Ultra led to the defeat of Rommel in North African. Just before the D-Day landings in June, 1944, the Allies knew the location of 56 of the 58 German divisions on the Western front.

The "main man" working at Bletchley Park was the mathematician, Alan Turing.

In 1950, Turing proposed a test to see if a machine (computer) could think and learn like a human. The test went something like this. A person engages in a natural language conversation with the machine. All participants are separated from each other. If the person cannot tell the machine from another human, the machine is said to have passed the Turing test.

Since 1950, the Turing test has come up constantly in the discussion of artificial intelligence. It has also been widely criticized. In order to exhibit intelligent behavior, the machine or computer must be able to learn, which means it must be able to change or modify its responses based on new information. It must be able to capture information, sift through it, and improve its response. That is what humans do.

Turing later proposed a test known as the Imitation Game. A man and woman go into separate rooms, and guests try to tell them apart by writing a series of questions and reading the typewritten answers sent back. Both the man and woman try to convince the guests they are the other. ELIZA and CAPTCHA are more modern natural language computer programs that aim to distinguish humans from computers.

Alan Turing died in 1954, just short of his 42nd birthday. The year 2012 was the 100th anniversary of Alan Turing's birth. The "father of computer science" was honored at Bletchley Park and Cambridge, England.

The cult classic science fiction movie "Blade Runner" starring Harrison Ford, which came out in 1982, depicts the Voight-Kampff test to distinguish humans from replicants. These bio-engineered robots have escaped and come back to Earth illegally. The replicants are supposed to have a four-year life, but they're trying to extend it. Wanting to live longer? Seems very human to me!

# Chapter Nine

# The Magnificent Atom

## Q81: *What is the size of an atom?*
. . . . . . . . . . . . . . . . . . . . . . . . . . . . . .

An atom is so small that a single drop of water contains more than a million, million, billion atoms. Atoms are so tiny that six million could fit on the period at the end of this sentence. Atoms are mostly empty space. The most accepted model of the atom is that of a cloud of negative electrons swarming in orbit around a tiny dense positive core called the nucleus. If a whole atom were the size of a professional football field, the nucleus would be a little pea out on the 50-yard line.

The Greek philosopher Democritus, in 500 BC, suggested that matter consisted of small indivisible particles which he called atoms. Our modern view of the atom is less than 100 years old and parts of the atom, such as the neutron, were not discovered until 1932.

The atom is defined to be the smallest part of an element that keeps the chemical properties of that element. There are about 92 naturally occurring elements, and around 118 when man-made elements are added in. The most plentiful atom in the universe is hydrogen. Elements up to iron, atomic number 26, are created in the stars. Elements heavier than iron are forged in supernova explosions.

We now know there is a whole menagerie of sub-atomic particles with strange names such as leptons, hadrons, quarks, muons, and baryons.

## Q82: *What happens when you split an atom?*
. . . . . . . . . . . . . . . . . . . . . . . . . . . . . . . . . . . . .

Splitting atoms releases a tremendous amount of energy. The process is called fission. Not just any old atom will work. It requires the right kind of atom, and uranium is the atom of choice. Uranium-235 is the most important atom in the production of nuclear power and atomic bombs. Uranium-235 is just on the verge of being unstable, so it doesn't take much to split it.

The number 235 is the sum of neutrons and protons in the nucleus or center of the atom. Protons have a positive charge and neutrons have no charge. The number of protons in the U-235 nucleus is 92, and is matched by the same number of negative electrons that swirl in orbits around the nucleus.

Uranium is a common element on Earth and has been around since the Earth was formed. The U-235 atoms "decays" or changes (transmutes) into another element all by itself by throwing off pieces of the nucleus. The most common is an alpha particle, which consists of 2 protons and 2 neutrons. This radioactivity is happening all the time. A handful of U-235 atoms would take billions of years to completely change, because there are a gazillion atoms in a handful.

But the fact that Uranium-235 could undergo changes provided scientists with a tantalizing clue in the late 1930's. What would happen if a neutron hit a U-235 nucleus? It has to be a neutron, because anything with a positive charge (proton) would be repelled by the positive protons in the nucleus. Like charges, such as a positive to a positive, repel each other.

In the late 1930s, three labs were racing to discover whether bombarding uranium with neutrons could lead to new elements: the Joliot-Curies lab in France, Enrico Fermi in Rome, The Lise Meitner-Hahn lab in Germany. If a neutron strikes a uranium nucleus at high speed, it goes right though the nucleus and comes out of the other side. Nothing happens. But if a neutron can be slowed down sufficiently before it hits the uranium nucleus, it will deform the nucleus and split it apart, giving two different elements, typically barium and krypton.

But here's the wonderful part. Along with the two new elements, at least two neutrons are released. These neutrons can split two other uranium atoms. And when these atoms split, a minimum of four neutrons split four uranium atoms. This cascading effect continues. We have a chain reaction. This process continues until all the U-235 atoms are split.

This is what happens in an atomic bomb. It is a runaway nuclear chain reaction. In the fission process, a tiny bit of mass is lost, and that lost mass goes into pure energy of blast, heat, and light. The equation that explains the equivalence between mass and energy is Albert Einstein's famous E equals mass times the speed of light squared. ($E = mc^2$) E is energy in joules, m is mass in kilograms, and c is the symbol for the speed of light in meters per second.

Nuclear fission in power plants, aircraft carriers, and submarines uses U-235, but the chain reaction is controlled. The rate of splitting atoms is slowed down tremendously.

Uranium found in nature is mostly U-238. Less than one percent is of the U-235 variety.

Natural uranium, a mixture of U-235 and U-238, can't be used for a bomb. The uranium for a bomb must be enriched to about 90 percent U-235, either by chemical means or by centrifuges.

The uranium used in power plants, on the other hand, is enriched to only about three percent. So a nuclear power plant cannot blow up like a nuclear bomb. However, the chain reaction can "get away from them," as witnessed at Three Mile Island and Chernobyl.

The bomb dropped on Hiroshima, Japan on August 6, 1945 was a uranium bomb. There are other atoms that can be split and other ways of making an atomic bomb. The plutonium from the spent fuel rods of a nuclear power plant can be processed and fashioned into a bomb like the one the United States dropped on Nagasaki a few days after Hiroshima. The bomb dropped on Nagasaki, Japan on August 9, 1945 was a plutonium bomb.

## Q83: How do scientists know the half-life of uranium is 4.5 billion years?

. . . . . . . . . . . . . . . . . . . . . . . . . . . . . . . . . . . . . . . . . . .

Radioactivity can't be seen, tasted, or felt. Radioactive elements become stable by throwing off particles or rays. Special instruments, called Geiger counters, detect alpha, beta, and gamma radiation. The half-life is the amount of time it takes for half the substance of a radioactive element to "decay" or change to another element.

Let's compare it to a classroom of 20 students. If 10 of them get the hiccups over a 14 day period, the hiccup half-life of the class is 14 days. Half-lives of elements range from fractions of a second to billions of years. So how can we determine the half-life of an element that is billions of years old? It turns out that the rate of radioactivity (how fast the Geiger counter ticks) is related to the half-life. An element like Uranium-238 has an extremely slow "click rate," so its half-life is billions of years. An element like radon clicks away like a blur at quite a fast rate and has a half-life of less than four days.

Our bodies contain at least three radioactive elements, Carbon-14, Potassium-40 (K-40), and Iodine-131. Not only does Carbon-14 occur naturally in the body, but Carbon-14 is also used as a tracer in medicine. Potassium-40 is necessary for growth and maintenance of the body. Our body has tiny amounts of Iodine-131, but the medical field also uses I-131 to scan the thyroid gland.

Every house has a tiny bit of radon gas. Radon is a gas that derives from the radioactive decay of radium. It is denser than air and settles to the lowest point possible. Radon gas detectors are available at most hardware and department stores and at very little cost. You can place the detector in a low place in the house for a period of time, such as 2 weeks. Then you mail the detector to a processing center, and soon you receive a written report of the results.

Ten million Americans are diagnosed using radioactive medicines yearly.

Technetium-99m is a gamma ray emitter, free of beta particles, and is widely used in a bevy of tests. Its six-hour half-life makes it ideal for hospital use.

## Q84: How are metals made?

Everything is made of atoms. The atom is the smallest piece of any pure substance. Any number of atoms makes up an element and each atom of any element is identical to the other atoms of that element.

Elements that occur in nature can be divided into metals and non-metals. Gold, copper, silver, and platinum are metals found in pure form. But most metals that we use in everyday life are alloys or mixtures of elements.

Alloys are made from two or more metals. Copper and tin are mixed to give us bronze. Copper and zinc create brass. Alloys are made by heating the elements until they form a liquid which can be mixed together. The liquid then cools and solidifies, and we get a new metal.

The wires in your house are made of copper, aluminum, iron, and zinc. Your plumbing pipes, if not polyvinyl chloride (PVC), are made from iron, chrome, manganese, zinc and carbon. You can use a magnet to hold pictures on your refrigerator door because of the iron in the door.

In nature, most metals are found in chemical combinations with non-metals. We call these combinations ores. The metals we want might be mixed with oxygen, sulfur, or carbon. To purify the metals, we heat the ore in a process called smelting.

Some metals are easy to get out and require heating to just the right temperature. Others, like iron, require mixing with carbon and heating in a blast furnace. Some, like aluminum, use a huge amount of electricity to free the aluminum atoms from the ore.

Metals are very good conductors of electricity and excellent conductors of heat. Metals are shiny because of the way they hold their electrons. The electrons are free to move about, so the atoms are able to absorb and reflect many different colors of light. This strong reflection makes the metals appear shiny.

Metals are heavy because they are organized into tightly packed repeating crystal patterns. Platinum is the heaviest metal, weighing about 21 times what water weighs. A gallon of milk weighs about 8.5 pounds, but a gallon of platinum weighs180 pounds. Gold and tungsten weigh about 19 times what water weighs.

## Q85: Why doesn't stainless steel rust like other metals?

S tainless steel contains iron, chromium, manganese, silicon, carbon and in some cases, nickel and molybdenum. The presence of those elements prevents iron oxide from forming.

The common term for iron oxide ($Fe_2 O_3$) is rust. Rusting is the reaction of iron and oxygen in the presence of water or any moisture. Rust is that reddish-brown color we see when iron or steel undergoes corrosion. Any iron mass will eventually convert entirely to rust and completely disintegrate given enough time, oxygen, and moisture.

The elements listed above react with the oxygen in water to form a very thin stable film over the underlying metal. This layer is thinner than a wavelength of light. It is so thin it cannot be seen by the eye or even by a light microscope. But this passive layer of corrosion is impervious to air and water and protects the metal underneath.

So indeed, stainless steel does "rust" into a protective barrier layer to make the iron or steel "stain less." Stainless steel has a high proportion of chromium compared to carbon. Advantage: The steel is less resistant to rusting. Disadvantage: Chromium makes the steel more brittle.

This idea of forming a passive corrosion protective layer is not unique to steel. Titanium and aluminum also rely on an extremely thin film formation to resist corrosion.

Because stainless steel does not rust, has great durability, and looks good, it is widely used in kitchen sinks, utensils, razor blades, vehicle trim, surgical instruments, and food-processing equipment. We see a lot of those 10,000 gallon stainless steel bulk tank trucks on the freeway.

Since most stainless steel is not magnetic it is used in magnetic resonance imaging (MRI) units in hospitals and clinics.

Stainless steel is a poor heat conductor. In contrast, copper is one of the best conductors of heat. But copper cookware is quite expensive and not found in too many home kitchens. That's why you often see stainless steel cookware with a copper bottom and stainless steel sides and top. Stainless steel pots and pans often have an inner core of aluminum or copper. There are trade-offs. Stainless steel cookware is cheaper, durable, and easy to clean, but not the very best material for cooking. Cooper is the best material for conducting heat, but it is expensive, reacts with acidic foods, and needs all that polishing.

Stainless steel conducts electricity, but much less well than gold, silver, copper, aluminum, steel, iron, or lead. You won't see stainless steel used in wiring.

## Q86: What is the strongest metal ever made?
· · · · · · · · · · · · · · · · · · · · · · · · · · · · · · · · · · · · · · ·

Tungsten, titanium, and Carbon-40 steel are all at the top of the chart. Keep in mind that there are several definitions of strongest. Hardness, tensile strength, impact resistance, and resistance to corrosion are properties that could describe what is "strongest." Even temperature makes a difference. Some metals become brittle when they're cold. Also, there are mixtures of metals, termed alloys, that make for some mighty strong materials.

Tungsten has one of the highest melting points known, at about 6,200 degrees Fahrenheit. The melting point is the temperature at which the metal goes from a solid to a liquid, i.e. melts. That makes tungsten useful as a filament in light bulbs and X-ray tubes.

Tungsten is brittle and hard to work with. Machining it is very difficult. Thomas Edison toyed with tungsten when he was trying to make the light bulb, but abandoned it. He just didn't have the tools he needed. Mixed with carbon, tungsten is even stronger. Some of the best drill bits we can buy are carbide tungsten.

Titanium also rates high as the strongest metal on earth. Titanium has a very high strength-to-weight ratio. It is strong, but light, and has a high melting temperature of about 3000 degrees Fahrenheit. High speed aircraft, such as the SR-71 spy plane, use titanium on the leading edges of the wings and fuselage. Compressor blades, casings, cowlings, pumps, valves, and heat shields on aircraft engines use titanium.

Titanium resists corrosion, making it useful for the metal finishing industry. Titanium is compatible with the human body, so many artificial hip, knee, and elbow joints are made with the metal. Titanium is put into pacemakers, defibrillators, and sunscreens.

Carbon-40 steel is iron alloyed with a tiny amount of carbon. Stainless steel contains chromium and nickel. Higher quality razor blades use stainless steel combined with a tiny amount of chromium. High strength steel has about 1.5 percent manganese added. Another strong alloy metal is 97% nickel, 2% beryllium, and less than one percent titanium. Inconel 625 is used in high-strength fasteners. Inconel, used for high temperature applications, is steel with small quantities of niobium and nickel added.

## Q87: Why does iron turn a red color when you heat it?

The old-time blacksmiths would heat up horseshoes and other iron implements. When the iron got hot enough, it glowed a dull red. As the iron got hotter, it turned orange-yellow, then bluish, and perhaps a bluish white.

The color or frequency of emitted light from an object is proportional to temperature. Early blacksmiths blew air into the flames to increase the efficiency of the fire. The extra air provided the fire with more oxygen, making it burn hotter.

The higher the temperature of an object, the higher the frequency of electromagnetic waves it emits. Frequency is the number of wave vibrations in a second.

Light is made of waves, just like water waves, except we can't see the individual waves as we can with water waves. Light consists of seven colors, easily remembered by using the memory aid ROYGBIV, which means red, orange, yellow, green, blue, indigo, and violet. Recall that it is really six colors, as indigo cannot easily be seen.

Red is the lowest-frequency (rate of vibration) wave we can see and violet is the highest. The waves of violet light have almost twice the frequency of red light waves. When the iron is white hot, it is radiating waves of all the colors put together, which of course, is white light.

The temperature of any incandescent body, whether a star or blast furnace, can be determined by measuring the frequency (color) of the light it emits. Old stars, such as Betelgeuse, located above the belt of Orion the Hunter, is a reddish, cool, older star. Rigel, located below the belt of Orion, is a young, hot, blue-colored star.

Waves that are very short can also be very dangerous. X rays and gamma rays can kill us or cure us. X-rays are invaluable diagnostic tools. Great care is exercised to confine the X-rays and steer them to prescribed points. Gamma rays are common tools in fighting cancer.

## Q88: Why is mercury poisonous?

A mercury spill at a local school prompted the question about the toxicity of mercury. Reports indicated a student brought a small plastic jar of mercury to school. A small amount of mercury spilled on the playground and on a carpet in the hallway. The principal acted quickly to cordon off the area and recover the mercury.

People have used mercury for over three thousand years. A mercury mine in Spain has been in continuous operation since the time of Christ. For centuries, criminals and slaves operated this mine. Today miners are allowed to work only 8 days a month, even if they wear protective clothing and masks.

Mercury is a gray metal that is a liquid at room temperature. It is over 13 times as dense as water. It is used in thermometers because it is an excellent conductor of heat. The mercury barometer is the most precise method of measuring the weight of the atmosphere. Mercury is used very safely in the amalgamation of metals for dental fillings.

No person should ever play with mercury. Metallic mercury is highly toxic by skin absorption and by inhalation of the vapors. As little as one hundredth of an ounce taken internally is lethal. The fumes are highly poisonous. Mercury was used in the millinery trade, or hat making, for many decades. The term "mad as a hatter" stems from the hideous neurological damage caused by prolonged exposure. Mercury can reside in our fatty tissues and stay there practically forever.

Mercury fumes are very unhealthy. The fumes can be detected by "sniffer tubes" which draw in a quantity of air and mix it with detecting reagents. A cheaper, but less accurate, method is to use indicator/detector cards treated with palladium chloride. The normally pink surface will turn gray in the presence of mercury vapor.

There are several approaches to cleaning up a mercury spill. Special sponges which contain an amalgamating powder, usually zinc, convert the toxic mercury to a metal/mercury amalgam. Environmental control companies rent powerful vacuum cleaners to help remove mercury from carpets, vents, and cracks. Never try to use a regular vacuum cleaner to pick up mercury. It won't work. Don't try to sweep it up with a broom. Ventilate the area by opening doors and windows. Push the pools of mercury together and put them into a container. Use an eyedropper to pick up some particles. Never dispose of mercury by putting it in the garbage or landfill. Call a chemical control officer.

Schools no longer use mercury in any science lab. Mercury thermometers are being replaced with red alcohol (hexane) thermometers. The red alcohol thermometers are slower-acting and not as accurate as mercury thermometers. But the health hazards of mercury thermometers far outweigh the drawbacks of alcohol thermometers.

## Q89: *What is air made of?*

Air is made of 21 percent oxygen, 78 percent nitrogen, and 1 percent inert gases and a bit of carbon dioxide. Inert means that these gases do not interact or mix with other materials. The inert gases are neon, argon, and xenon. It may seem strange, but oxygen, the stuff that we need to keep us alive, is only a small fraction of what we breathe. What we don't seem to need is the nitrogen.

Many people think that air does not weigh anything. But air does have weight, and it exerts a force of 14.7 pounds of pressure on every square inch of the Earth's surface.

In the 1650s, Otto von Guericke of Magdeburg, Germany, devised a striking experiment to show the enormous force the atmosphere can exert on a container from which the air has been pumped. He made two hollow hemispheres about 22 inches in diameter. The edges were ground so smoothly that when they were coated with heavy grease, they fit together airtight. He then took the air out of the hemispheres with his newly invented vacuum pump and closed the stopcock. It took 16 horses, eight on each side, to pull the hemispheres apart.

A simple calculation of area (380 square inches) multiplied by 14.7 pounds per square inch, yields a force of over 5500 lbs. of pull that each side (eight horses) would have to exert to separate the hemispheres.

Most of us have no problem blowing up a balloon. When we inflate a balloon, the balloon pushes air out of the way. Now, try this real challenge! Push the bottom of the balloon into a pop bottle and stretch the top of the balloon over the mouth of the bottle.

Try to inflate the balloon. Notice that the balloon is only partly inflated. Why? The pop bottle is already filled with air. So blowing into the balloon makes the air molecules inside the bottle squeeze closer together, but only slightly. The air is in the way of the balloon and prevents it from inflating.

## Q90: What is water made of?

· · · · · · · · · · · · · · · · · · · · · · · · ·

The short answer: two hydrogen atoms bonded to one oxygen atom forms a molecule of water. A drop of water contains billions of molecules of water. But there is more complexity to water.

Water is known as a universal solvent. Acids, sugars, salts, and alkalis all dissolve in water. All parts inside the cell, such as protein and DNA, dissolve in water.

Water is odorless, tasteless, and has a slight bluish tint in large quantities. Small quantities, such as a handful, appear colorless. Water covers 70 percent of the Earth's surface. Less than three percent of the Earth's water is fresh and most of that, 98 percent, is in ice and groundwater.

Water has its greatest density at 39 degrees Fahrenheit (4

degrees Centigrade or Celsius). Water becomes less dense as it cools down to 32 degrees Fahrenheit, the temperature at which it freezes to form ice. As water freezes, it expands about 9 percent in volume, making it less dense. For this reason, ice floats in water.

Water has a very slight negative charge and so can form a large number of bonds with other molecules, which leads to a high surface tension and capillary action. Surface tension permits skeeter bugs to walk on water. It is capillary action that permits water to rise up more than 300 feet in a giant sequoia tree.

Pure water will not conduct electricity, but any impurities, such as salt or soap or minerals, anything with ions, will increase the conductivity. So don't drop your radio or hair curler in the bathtub while you are in it.

Substances that do not mix are said to be immiscible. Water will not mix with fats and oils and will form in layers, with the least dense layer on top.

If water is made up of hydrogen and oxygen, can a water molecule be taken apart? Yes, the process is called electrolysis. Direct current (DC) can break water into two gases, hydrogen and oxygen. These two gases can be cooled down into liquids, in which form they are widely used in hospitals, welding, and rocket fuels.

Water has the highest heat value or capacity of any common liquid or solid. Simply put, hot water will give off a lot of heat, and it takes a lot of heat to make water hot. So water is very good in a car radiator to keep the engine cool. Water acts as a temperature moderator, preventing great changes in the Earth's temperatures.

Pure water does not taste good. It's the dissolved minerals in water that gives it the good taste you and I prefer. Bottled water has all those good minerals, but not the pollutants, toxins, and microbes we don't want. Astronauts on Mercury, Gemini, and

Apollo flights got their drinking water from fuel cells. Fuel cells mix oxygen and hydrogen to make electricity. A byproduct is pure water, which serves as drinking water. It tasted so bad the astronauts mixed Tang orange juice with water so as to give it taste.

On average, ocean or sea water is about 4 percent salts. Incidentally, that's about the same percent of salt that is in our blood. Our body is about 75 percent water. We can survive without food for three weeks, but only one week without water.

## Q91: If hydrogen and oxygen are gases, how can they make water?

Water is made when two hydrogen atoms attach to an oxygen atom. This occurs naturally. The orbits of each atom's electrons are linked. It would be dangerous to take massive amounts of oxygen and hydrogen gases and bring them together to form water. Hydrogen gas is flammable and oxygen supports combustion. The ill-fated Hindenburg airship was filled with hydrogen gas when it blew up in New Jersey in 1937.

Yet, it is possible to combine hydrogen and oxygen gases to make water. This occurs in a fuel cell. An additional byproduct of a fuel cell is the production of electricity. Fuel cells were used in the space program to put men on the moon. Today there is a lot of research to make hydrogen-powered cars.

It is much easier to go the other way and take water to make oxygen and hydrogen gases. This separation of water into its two component elements is called electrolysis. Any battery tied to conducting rods and stuck in water will produce oxygen and hydrogen gases.

Water is the one chemical substance that is needed for the survival of all known forms of life. Water has been called the universal solvent. A solvent is a liquid that can dissolve another substance. Water is a polar molecule. Oxygen attracts electrons more strongly than hydrogen does, so there is a net positive charge on the hydrogen and a net negative charge on the oxygen atom. This type of molecule, with regions of positive charge and regions of negative charge, can attract other molecules and tear them apart. Salt, NaCl, which has its own attractive forces that hold it together, can be dissolved.

Typically, we experience water as a liquid. But water freezes to a solid, ice, at 0 degrees Celsius and evaporates or boils and turns into steam or vapor at 100 degrees Celsius. These changes from a solid to a liquid to a gas or from a gas to a liquid to a solid are called phase changes. When substances such as water change phase, their physical properties change. However, their chemical properties do not. Melting, freezing, condensation, and evaporation are examples of phase changes. The phase of a substance depends on temperature and pressure.

Water has a polarity feature. As mentioned above, oxygen atoms are slightly negative, and hydrogen has a slight positive charge. This polarity creates strong enough bonds to keep the molecule from flying apart at room temperature. We have a liquid instead of a gas.

Antoine Lavoisier, often called the father of modern chemistry, is credited with the discovery of oxygen and hydrogen, and actually determined that water consisted of one part oxygen and two parts hydrogen. Lavoisier also compiled the first modern list of chemicals and introduced the metric system. He was wrongly accused of treason and beheaded in 1794 during the French Revolution.

## Q92: Why is water wet?
. . . . . . . . . . . . . . . . . . .

The short answer is that water is a liquid, but that is not a very accurate or even satisfying answer. Some liquids, such as mercury, don't feel wet.

In order for a liquid to feel wet, it must spread out and stick to your skin. Water is made of hydrogen and oxygen or $H_2O$. But oxygen and hydrogen don't share their electrons equally when they form a bond. The oxygen atom carries a negative charge and the hydrogen atom has a slight positive charge. Water is known as a polar molecule.

Water molecules exhibit cohesion—a natural attraction to themselves. Cohesion is what holds water molecules together to make a water drop. Other polar molecules can break the cohesiveness of water molecules by exerting their own attractive electrical force. This is called adhesion. Your skin has a strong adhesive force to water that overcomes the force of attraction of water molecules to other water molecules. Some of the water molecules adhere, or stick to your hand, making it feel wet.

Try this simple science experiment. Spill some water on your table top and hold the end of a paper towel in water. Notice that the water creeps up the paper towel a distance of several inches in just a few minutes. You are watching capillary action or the rising of liquids in small diameter tubes. The spaces between the paper fibers act as tubes. Adhesion and cohesion act together to raise or elevate the water level.

## Q93: *Why does hot water freeze faster than cold water?*

It seems to be a contradiction to say that hot water can freeze faster than cold water. The great scientist, Francis Bacon, was one of the first to write about the phenomenon. People in northern climates, especially in Canada, are well aware of this condition.

The critical factor here is the increased evaporation from the initially warmer water. Evaporation occurs when water as a liquid turns into invisible vapor. The containers must be open-topped and have a large surface area. The evaporation of the hot water decreases the mass of the water in that container. With less mass to cool, the water in that container can overtake the cooling of the cold water and reach the freezing point first.

Several other factors can help hot water freeze first. Air movement above the containers and slight circulation of the water both aid in the effect. The amount of heat energy, in calories, required to heat an object or given off by a cooling object, depends on the mass, the specific heat, and the change in temperature. The specific heat of water is one. It takes one calorie to heat 1 gram of water 1 degree Celsius.

Try this simple science experiment. Place two dinner plates in your freezer. Pour hot water in one and cold water in the other. Make sure the same amount of water is poured onto each plate.

Close your freezer, but check on the plates every ten minutes. Does the hot water freeze first? It should. The ideal situation would be to carry out this experiment outdoors in winter weather.

## Q94: *How do diamonds form?*

Diamonds form under tremendous heat and pressure. These conditions occur about one hundred miles below the Earth's surface in a layer called the mantle.

Diamonds are made of pure carbon. The arrangement of these atoms is known as an isometric-hexoctahedral crystal lattice. That is a term that says all the atoms are arranged in a regular manner and all are attached to each other in the same fashion. It is this arrangement of the atoms that makes diamonds a thousand times stronger than rubies or sapphires. This array of atoms gives diamonds extreme hardness, luster, and ability to conduct heat.

A diamond has a very high refractive index, which means it can bend light better than any known substance. It is this quality that makes diamonds useful in jewelry. The dazzling display creates "a girl's best friend." But only about twenty percent of diamonds go into jewelry. The majority of diamonds are used by industry to make cutting tools, to polish hard metal surfaces, and to make ball bearings in lab equipment.

People sometimes associate diamonds with coal. Coal was formed by vegetative and animal material in the crust of the Earth close to the surface. Diamonds were formed before there were plants and animals on Earth. Diamonds work their way to the Earth's surface through pipes and vents during volcanic eruptions. Those pipes and channels contain the magma from volcanoes. The diamonds rise along with the magma to near the Earth's surface, where they are later found and mined.

Also, coal is found in seams of sedimentary rock, in horizontal layers. Diamonds are found in igneous rock in vertical pipes or vents.

The first diamonds were found in India in the 1720s. During our Civil War, diamonds were found in large numbers in South

Africa. That is where most of the world's diamonds come from today.

The largest diamond ever found is the Cullinan Diamond discovered in 1905 in South Africa. It weighed 3,106 carats. A carat is one-fifth of a gram. The average paper clip is one gram. A dollar bill weighs a gram.

The Cullinan Diamond weighed 620 grams or a tad less than 1.5 pounds. It was cut into 9 large diamonds and about 100 small ones. The value of a diamond is based on the four c's: carats, cut, clarity, and color.

Diamonds come in almost any color. The most common colors are white, yellow, and brown. Diamonds can also be blue, red, orange, or purple. A very brightly colored diamond is called a fancy.

Well, fancy that!

# Chapter Ten

# More Things
# I Always
# Wondered About

## Q95: *If you are in a falling elevator, can you save yourself by jumping up just before it hits ground level?*

. . . . . . . . . . . . . . . . . . . . . . . . . . . . . . . . . . . . . . . . . . .

A fine question and one that people have debated for many years. Good luck, but if the elevator falls any significant distance, jumping up will not likely save your life.

First of all, if a cable has broken, you would be in free fall and floating around inside the elevator, much like the astronauts in the International Space Station. They are in constant free fall. There is only a slight chance your feet will be in contact with the floor at the moment the elevator hits the bottom of the shaft. But let's say your feet are 'velcroed' to the floor and you can somehow anticipate the proper time to jump upward.

Pretend the elevator falls ten floors, or about 120 feet. You would be going about 88 feet per second or 60 miles per hour. Let's assume you can normally jump up in the air a distance of four feet. (Only a few basketball players have a four-foot standing jump). You would jump upward at 16 feet per second or about ten miles per hour. So, if you subtract the 10 mph from the 60 mph, you're still slamming into the ground at 50 mph. Now remember, most of us can't jump up a distance of four feet. We're lucky to do two feet. So don't count on saving yourself in a falling elevator by jumping up at the last second. It will not work, either for you or the star forward of the LA Lakers.

Not to worry, however. If the elevator cable breaks, safety devices will stop the elevator from falling. Elisha Otis invented the safety elevator in 1885 for the ten-story Home Insurance Company skyscraper in Chicago.

Larry Scheckel

## Q96: Why are rockets launched to the east, and why are they always launched from Florida?

It takes a speed of 17,000 miles per hour to get anything into Earth orbit. The Earth is about 25,000 miles all the way around. It takes 24 hours for the Earth to make one rotation. Divide that circumference of 25,000 miles by 24 hours and you get a rough figure of 1,000 miles per hour.

So a launch pad at the equator is already going 1000 miles per hour to the East due to the rotation of the Earth. A rocket fired eastward gets a free "kick in the pants" and thus needs less fuel. Florida is about as close to the equator as the U.S. gets.

Yes, California has better weather and is almost as far south as Florida. But launching East from Florida takes the rockets over the Atlantic, so any explosion, such as the Shuttle Challenger explosion in January, 1986, will result in debris falling into the water. Also, the solid rocket boosters are picked up in the Atlantic.

Launching east from California would put the flight path over land. California, Arizona, New Mexico, and Texas would have rockets passing overhead. You wouldn't want to live in Phoenix, Arizona and look up and see rocket rubble falling on you!!

Vandenberg Air Force Base in California launches rockets in a southern direction for satellites that travel over the poles. The Pacific Ocean would receive any rocket parts falling earthward. Some of our spy satellites are launched from Vandenberg AFB.

The Space Shuttle program has ended, but the United States continues to send payloads into earth orbit and geosynchronous orbit. The Delta 4 can put 50,000 pounds into space, and the Atlas 5 can lift 64,000 pounds. Both rockets are sent aloft from the Cape Kennedy complex and from Vandenberg AFB.

The NASA facility at Wallops Island, Virginia has become a major player in rocket launching. Payloads to the International

Space Station and from private companies are being sent aloft from the barrier island on the Atlantic coast.

The European Space Agency, formed in 1975, launch their craft from French Guiana on the northern tip of South America. Their spaceport is very close to the equator, at only five degrees north latitude. It is an ideal spot for launches into low earth orbit and the higher geosynchronous orbit.

### Q97: If you are weightless in space, would you be able to pick up heavy objects?

Objects in space may be weightless, but they still have mass. And it requires a force to move that mass. Newton's Second Law of Motion is the relationship between mass, force, and acceleration: $F = ma$. $F$ is force, $m$ is mass, and the letter $a$ stands for acceleration. This law applies on earth and in space.

Objects on the former space shuttle, and now on the International Space Station, may weigh hundreds of pounds. In space, you could easily hold that mass in your hand. But if you want to move it, you must apply a force. A force is simply a push or a pull.

Once you get an object moving, say from the floor to the ceiling, it will continue to move "up" until you apply a force to stop it. If you don't apply a force to stop it, the object will hit the ceiling.

Astronauts use a foot restraint system. Canvas loops are taped to the floor, and astronauts slide their feet into the loops. When the astronauts are space walking outside their craft, their boots have a lip on the back of the shoe that locks into foot restraints. Foot restraints are placed on the floor, doors, and ceilings.

The foot restraints allow the astronaut to apply some leverage to whatever they are trying to move, lift, or manipulate. The restraints anchor the astronaut in place. They substitute for the weight that you and I have, that gives us anchorage here on Earth.

The term weightlessness is somewhat misleading and implies that there is no gravity in space. In fact, the pull of gravity in Earth orbit is almost identical to the force of gravity on the surface of the Earth. The previous shuttle and now the International Space Station and the astronauts inside are actually in a state of free fall.

Let's say you stand on a bathroom scale and jump off a building. On the way down, you read the scale. You are weightless and in free fall, and the scale reads zero. Space is the same way. When in Earth orbit, the spacecraft and astronaut are moving forward and falling downward at the same time. The fall of the International Space Station and the astronauts inside matches the curvature of the Earth.

## Q98: Why does glue stick?

This is a simple question with a complex answer. The short answer is that there is a molecular attraction between the glue and the material to which it is applied. Adhesion is the force of attraction between unlike molecules. Most adhesives are liquid to start with because they must be in close contact with the materials being glued.

Adhesion occurs at the molecular level. Glues and adhesives involve Van der Waals forces. Molecules are polarized. They have very weak negative and positive ends. The two hydrogen atoms of a water molecule are slightly skewed to one side, at an angle of about 104 degrees. Opposites attract, so the positive side of one water molecule will be attracted to the negative side of the one next to it. That is the Van der Waals force.

Say you break the handle off your coffee cup. In order for the two surfaces to adhere, they must be within a few millionths of an inch of each other. Most solid surfaces are too rough to allow more than a tiny amount of their surface area to be that close. A liquid glue can flow into those surface irregularities and provide the close contact.

Surfaces that are smooth and clean can adhere spontaneously. There was fear in the early years of the space program that the shiny metal boots of the astronauts might stick to the smooth surface of the spacecraft. Spontaneous adhesion is observed when layers of mica are separated by a knife and pressed together again.

Post-it® Notes, using a temporary adhesive, were invented by a Minnesota Mining and Manufacturing (3M) scientist in St. Paul to mark the pages in his church music book. One of the earliest known glues was beeswax and tar. These glues go back to biblical times. Carpenter's glue was made from leftover slaughterhouse pieces of bones and hides.

You might give this a try. Find two heavy plastic water glasses. Put one inside the other and drip water around the rim of the outer glass so that a thin layer of water forms between the two glasses.

Try to put them apart. The water acts as glue holding the glasses together. The force of adhesion and cohesion are at work here. To get the two glasses apart, put cold water in the inner glass and run hot water around the outer glass. Cold water makes glass shrink and hot water makes glass expand.

## Q99: *Why are rivers so curvy?*

. . . . . . . . . . . . . . . . . . . . . . . . .

It would seem logical and natural for a river to run straight. Rivers that flow over gentle sloping ground do begin to curve back and forth. Such rivers are predictably called meandering rivers. Meanders are caused by erosion and sediment deposit.

Due to some asymmetry or obstruction in the river bed, such as rocks, weed growth, or fallen trees, the speed of the flowing water between the two banks differs. On the faster side of the river, less sediment is deposited. And because the water is flowing faster, more erosion takes place. At the slower side of the river, more sediment from erosion is deposited. Slower moving water has more time for the soil particles to settle out.

You can see what happens here. The faster moving water eats into the bank, making a small curve. Once the curve is established, the water on the outside of the curve must travel faster than on the inside. Thus the outside of the curve becomes more eroded. The river erodes soil from the outer curve and deposits on the inner curve. This causes the meanders to grow larger and larger. The bend gets more and more pronounced with time. The slower side of the river will continue to get slower while the faster side gets faster. Thus more sediment gets deposited on the slow side and more erosion happens on the fast side.

This process continues until the curves are so sharp the river will eventually cut through a curve and reestablish a straight path. This most often occurs at a time of flooding. The cut-off part of the river forms an oxbow, named for the part of the yoke for oxen. It could be viewed as a pronounced U-shaped bend in the river. Over years, many oxbows will fill in with sediments and plant growth.

From a high vantage point, one can see the oxbows from decades past. Some newly formed oxbows will harbor water for years and form lakes if large enough. Crater Lake, Iowa was created in 1877 after severe flooding shifted the Missouri River over a mile to the southeast.

The town of Horseshoe Lake, Arkansas is built on the eastern tip of a U-shaped body of water. Changes in the course of the Mississippi River created an oxbow. The lake is no longer connected to the Mississippi River.

The low-lying area around a river is termed a flood plain. Sediment is deposited after heavy rains and spring flooding, yielding some very rich land for crops.

We had a few acres of that kind of farmland down in Kettle Hollow on the Oak Grove Ridge farm in the heart of Crawford County, in southwestern Wisconsin. The soil was so rich that if you dropped a seed corn in a small furrow and covered it up, you had to get your head out of the way, lest the fast-growing stalk hit you in the face. Wow! That is rich farmland!

## Q100: Why is Chicago known as the Windy City?

There are several theories as to the origin of the "Windy City" nickname. One source goes back as far as 1876 when Cincinnati and Chicago were bidding for the 1893 Columbian Exposition, a sort of World's Fair. Cincinnati proponents claimed that the Chicago people were a bit "windy" in their claims, which means they exaggerated a lot. Chicago did win the bid to host the event in commemoration of the 400th anniversary of Christopher Columbus' discovery of the New World.

There also was a fierce baseball rivalry between the "Cincinnati Red Stockings" and the "Chicago White Stockings" in the late 1860's. The Cincinnati newspapers often referred to their "windy" opponents in the 1870's and 1880's.

A second possibility of the origin of the name "Windy City" is that Chicago is on Lake Michigan, and the wind frequently comes off the lake at a brisk pace.

A third "windy city" explanation was put forth by an Albert Lea, Minnesota newspaperman in the 1992. He expounded on the Chicagoan tendency to be "braggarts." He also talked about the effects of tall buildings channeling the winds down the narrow streets.

The windiest city in the United States is actually Cheyenne, Wyoming with an average wind speed of 12.8 miles per hours, followed by Great Falls, Montana, with a wind speed of 11.9 miles per hour. For large cities, Boston tops the list with a wind speed of 12.3 miles per hour. Milwaukee is fourth in the nation for large cities at 11.5 miles per hour. Chicago is ranked 21st of the 68 windiest cities, with an average wind speed of 10.3 miles per hour.

The highest wind speed ever recorded was in the White Mountains of New Hampshire. A speed of 231 miles per hour was recorded atop Mount Washington on April 12, 1934.

Tornadoes and hurricanes attest to the destructiveness of wind. But wind also has been a faithful servant of mankind. Wind filled the sails of ships for centuries, turned mills that pumped water for more than 3,000 years, and now moves blades to generate electricity. Wind allows for the sports of hang gliding, kite flying, and windsurfing.

Wind has played a role in warfare. The divine wind, or kamikaze, was a typhoon that saved Japan from the invasion fleets under Mongolian Kublai Khan in 1274 and 1281. A strong wind played a decisive role in protecting England from the invading Spanish Armada in 1588. Favorable winds helped

William of Orange invade England in 1688.

Who is the windiest politician? Well, that's a matter of opinion and probably depends on your political persuasion. But it was said that a former U.S. senator could speak 300 words per minute, with gusts up to 350!

## Q101: Why do tall buildings in big cities have revolving doors?

Revolving doors serve as an airlock, which keeps cold air out, thereby reducing heating costs. Revolving doors cut off the air path between the outside of the building and the inside.

Revolving doors are important in buildings that have an elevator. Let's suppose we have an open door at street level. There is an air path from outside, through the open door, through the elevator doors, up the elevator shaft, out the vents into the machine room, and out of the building. Revolving doors act as a draft block, preventing this chimney effect of sucking air in at high speeds and ejecting it through vents in the roof.

So the main reasons for using revolving doors are energy efficiencies in heating and cooling and preventing drafts. But there are other advantages. Revolving doors allow large numbers of people to pass in and out easily and quickly. These doors permit people to enter and exit at the same time. Most revolving doors can accommodate strollers and those wheeled luggage bags. Revolving doors block much street noise from entering a building. The noise created by a hinged door opening and closing is eliminated. Car and bus fumes are locked out. Hinged or swinging doors can create a wind that is strong enough to blow small objects around. Revolving doors prevent that strong draft.

Architects love revolving doors as they make a building more aesthetically pleasing due to the size of the doors. There is a psychological effect at work. The space between the panels of the revolving door is quite small. When a person steps out of the door, the room they are standing in automatically seems larger than it really is.

People carrying packages also love revolving doors. Both hands are free. These doors are ideal for accommodating people on crutches or in wheel chairs. Revolving doors usually have glass panels, which allow people to see and anticipate who is coming and going.

Revolving doors can be used for security purposes, involving radiation detectors and metal detectors. Sensors can go off it a person tries to enter in the wrong direction.

Large revolving door systems may have, in the central pivot, a small glass enclosure permitting the display of sculptures, mannequins, plants, or advertisements.

The revolving door was invented and patented by Theophilus Van Kannel of Philadelphia in 1888. The world's first revolving door was installed in a restaurant in New York's Times Square ten years later.

Most countries have right-hand traffic patterns, so most revolving doors rotate counter-clockwise as seen from above. People can enter and exit only on the right side of the door. Rotation direction is mandated by a governor or by the sealing between the door and the frame. Exceptions are Australia and New Zealand, where people not only walk on the wrong side, but also drive on the wrong side of the street!

I Always Wondered About That

**Larry Scheckel** grew up on a family farm in the hill country of southwestern Wisconsin, one of nine children. He attended eight years of a one room country school. After serving in the military and working as an engineer, he taught high school physics and æronautics for thirty-eight years. He has won numerous teaching awards, authored many articles, and given presentations on science to thousands of adults and young people. Now retired from teaching, Larry enjoys bicycling, flying real and radio-controlled airplanes, and solving crossword puzzles. Larry and his wife, Ann, live in Tomah, Wisconsin, and love to travel.

## Books by Larry Scheckel

*Ask A Science Teacher (2011)*

*Ask Your Science Teacher (2013)*

*Seneca Seasons: A Farm Boy Remembers (2014)*

*I've Always Wondered About That: 101 Questions and Answers About Science and Other Stuff (2017)*

*Murder in Wisconsin Hill Country: The 1926 Clara Olson Case (pending 2018)*